180
Devotions
for
WHEN LIFE
IS HARD

180
Devotions
for
WHEN LiFE
IS HARD

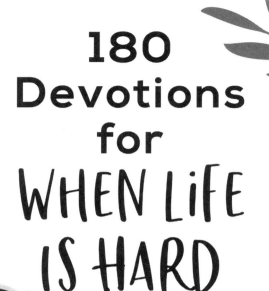

ENCOURAGEMENT
FOR A
TEEN GIRL'S HEART

Rae Simons

BARBOUR
PUBLISHING

Published by Barbour Publishing, Inc., 1810 Barbour Drive, Uhrichsville, Ohio 44683, www.barbourbooks.com

Our mission is to inspire the world with the life-changing message of the Bible.

Printed in the United States of America.

INTRODUCTION

Even when life is hard, God is with you. You can count on His love. He will never ever abandon you.

The Bible is full of messages of love from God. This book will give you a sample of those love messages. Each day, you'll read a brief Bible passage that will help you understand God and His love a little better. It may also challenge you to live your life a little differently. Next, you'll spend a few moments meditating on the truths found in the Bible passage, allowing them to take root in your mind. Finally, you can respond in prayer, turning your time with the Bible into a two-way conversation with God. This three-part structure—Bible reading, meditation, prayer—is a good way to come to God whenever life is hard.

God loves *you* so much, and He wants to use you to carry His message of love to others.

GENERATION GAP

*The glory of the young is their strength; the gray
hair of experience is the splendor of the old.*

PROVERBS 20:29 NLT

The expression "generation gap" was first used in the 1960s. Before that, in most cultures around the world, people didn't see a "gap" between young people and older people. Adults didn't feel as though young people were some new species of alien they couldn't understand, and young people didn't look at grown-ups as being too old to be of any real use.

The thing is—every adult you know was once your age. And one day you will be the age of every adult you know. Everyone falls somewhere on the same timeline between birth and death, and each stage has its own joys and strengths. So enjoy the age you are now, but be open to learning from people who are older than you are. You can learn something from everyone you know, no matter what their age is.

. . . .

*Father God, sometimes it seems as though the adults
in my life just don't understand me at all. When I feel
like that, remind me to try to understand them. May
Your love help us cross any gap we feel between us.*

LOOKING GOOD

*Humans are satisfied with whatever looks
good; GOD probes for what is good.*
PROVERBS 16:2 MSG

If you're like most girls your age, you want to look good. You want hair and clothes that are both stylish and flattering. You want your body to be fit and strong. God wants you to feel good about your appearance, but He cares more about the inner you. He wants you to be beautiful emotionally, mentally, and spiritually. He wants you to interact with others in a way that makes both you and them feel good. So it's okay to want to look good, but remember that God wants to shine through every bit of you, including your feelings, your thoughts, your conversations, and your prayers.

. . . .

*Teach me, Lord, to rely more on You for
my beauty than on clothes or hairstyle or
makeup. Make me glow with Your love!*

BE YOURSELF!

We justify our actions by appearances;
GOD examines our motives.
PROVERBS 21:2 MSG

Sure, you want to look good to others. But trying to look good isn't always about your physical appearance. Sometimes you might try to impress other people by bragging about something you're good at. You might want to look good by showing off. Sometimes, because you want someone to be nice to you, you might be afraid to say no, and then you end up in situations where you're not comfortable. Or you might try to prove what a good person you are by getting good grades or being involved in every after-school activity that comes along. There's certainly nothing wrong with being nice to people or working hard to earn good grades or participating in a lot of different things, but remember—you never have to earn God's approval. He cares a whole lot more about your motives than He does about any of your achievements, no matter how impressive they may be.

. . . .

Remind me, Lord God, not to worry so much
about what people think of me. I want
Your love to free me to just be me!

SCARED!

*"For I am the Lord your God who takes
hold of your right hand and says to
you, Do not fear; I will help you."*

Isaiah 41:13 NIV

Do you ever wake up feeling scared about the day
ahead? Maybe you have a big exam. . .or you have to
give an oral presentation. . .or you've made up your
mind to stop going along with things you feel are
wrong. Being scared is a normal human reaction, but
whenever you feel afraid, God wants you to know He's
right there with you. If you let Him, He'll lead you in
the right direction. He'll be with you as you take your
exam, as you do your presentation, and as you speak up
for what's right. You never have to do anything alone.

. . . .

*When I'm scared, Father, remind me that
You are close beside me. Teach me to rely
on Your love to make me strong.*

THE REAL you

The Lord directs our steps, so why try to understand everything along the way?
PROVERBS 20:24 NLT

Do you ever get tired of trying to make everyone happy with you? Your parents expect one set of things from you, your teachers and coaches want other things, and your friends expect you to talk and act in other ways. Trying to meet all these expectations can get confusing—and exhausting. You might even feel like there are three (or more) separate "yous": your parents think you're one person, your teachers and coaches think you're someone else, and your friends see a different person altogether. But God always sees the *real* you, the you who lives in the deepest, most private part of you. As you learn to follow God, He will help you in every situation to be true to that "you" He loves so much.

When I feel confused about who I am, remind me to take time to get to know the real me, the me You know and love, Lord.

NEW ADVENTURES

*The LORD will be your confidence and will
keep your foot from being caught.*
PROVERBS 3:26 NRSV

As you grow older, new opportunities are opening up
to you. Learning to drive, being entrusted with more
responsibilities, gaining more freedom—those are all
exciting things. But with each one comes risks. You may
feel nervous about all these new experiences, even
though you're looking forward to them. Sometimes
you might worry that you'll fail, that you won't be
smart enough or strong enough or talented enough
to live up to these new challenges. Those feelings are
normal; every person who has gone through adolescence
has had them. As you head into new adventures,
God wants to share both your excitement and your
nervousness. You can trust Him to stay with you, no
matter what happens.

*So many new and exciting things lie ahead, Lord.
I can't wait to experience them all. Give me Your
strength, Your love, and Your confidence so that
I can sail smoothly into these new adventures.*

ALL THINGS IN MODERATION

Do you like honey? Don't eat too much, or it will make you sick!
PROVERBS 25:16 NLT

You could apply this verse to your diet—eating too many sugary snacks isn't good for you in either the short term or the long term—but I suspect the wise author of the book of Proverbs was also talking about something besides food. He was saying you need to be careful not to overdo things; you need to practice moderation. This means you don't exercise so much that you make yourself sick; you don't diet until you're light-headed from low blood sugar; you don't hang out with your friends, laughing and talking, so much that you don't have time for your homework; and you don't spend so much time on your homework that you don't have any chance to enjoy being with your friends! Focusing too much on any one area of life can mean that other parts of your life don't get the attention they need. God wants your life to be balanced and healthy.

* * *

Show me, Father God, the way to live a balanced life. Give me Your wisdom so that I can make smart decisions.

MAKE A DIFFERENCE!

By the blessing of the upright a city is exalted.
PROVERBS 11:11 NRSV

"What does this verse mean?" you may be asking. "Why should I care about exalting a city?" The word that is translated as "city," though, had a slightly different meaning in the original language in which the Bible was written. It had to do with a group of people working together—in other words, a community. So what this verse is really saying is this: you have the power to make a difference in your neighborhood, city, state, nation, and even the entire world.

Around the world, young people your age are standing up to speak out on many different issues that concern the entire human community—things like the environment, education, and justice. But you don't have to address the United Nations or make a speech at a political rally. What you believe about life, how you express those beliefs, and how you treat your friends, family, and other people in your life can have a bigger impact than you realize. God can use your life, even in little ways, to bless the communities in which you live.

. . . .

Use me, Lord God, to make a difference in the world. Show me where You might want me to volunteer. Help me to always speak up for truth, justice, and love.

BOUNDARIES

*"I [Wisdom] was there when he set the
limits of the seas, so they would not
spread beyond their boundaries."*

PROVERBS 8:29 NLT

Being wise isn't about being smart; people who have
intellectual challenges can be wiser than the world's
smartest scientist. Wisdom has to do with practicing
love in every aspect of life. In the book of Proverbs,
the author speaks of Wisdom (with a capital *W*) as a
woman. This wonderful woman was with God when
the world was made. Wisdom watched with joy as He
drew boundaries around the oceans to protect His
other creations from drowning.

In your own life, Wisdom will help you know where
to set healthy boundaries. Establishing boundaries is
part of loving yourself. No one has a right to step over
your boundary lines and take advantage of you—not
your friends, not your boyfriend, not your family. No
one! God created you to be a unique and wonderful
individual, and Wisdom will teach you how to lovingly
guard the beautiful identity God gave you.

. . . .

*Father God, I ask for Your wisdom so that
I'll know where to set the boundaries that
will protect my body, mind, and heart.*

WORK

The diligent find freedom in their work.
PROVERBS 12:24 MSG

Does work feel like freedom to you? Whether we're talking about your schoolwork, the chores you do at home, the practice you put in for a sport or musical instrument, or an after-school job, does doing it give you a sense of joy and fun, or do you feel weighed down by the work? When you do this work, are you bored, frustrated, or resentful? God wants you to enjoy your work, so if you're not, maybe you need to stop and think about what's wrong. You might need to talk to your parents, teachers, or guidance counselor and get their advice. It could be that your schedule is overloaded and you need to drop something from it. Or maybe you just need to be patient and keep working. God wants you to have freedom in your work.

. . . .

Help me, Lord, to take a good look at the work I do. Show me if something needs to go—and show me also if there's an area where I need to work harder. I want to experience Your freedom in the work I do.

ANGER

Fools vent their anger, but the wise quietly hold it back.
PROVERBS 29:11 NLT

You may have gotten the idea that getting angry is wrong. Girls, especially, are encouraged to be "nice" and not get mad. Feeling angry doesn't automatically mean you've done something displeasing to God, though. Anger is a normal and healthy response to something that's not fair. Look at Jesus when He got mad at the sellers who were cheating people in the temple (Matthew 21:12). Jesus was so angry, He tipped over the money changers' tables. He took a loud and determined stand against something that wasn't fair.

But anger can also make you do things that hurt others. So before you tip any tables over, ask God to show you the best way to express your anger. Take time to think and pray.

. . . .

*Jesus, I like knowing that You got angry sometimes.
Thank You that You were as human as I am. Teach
me how to listen to the Father the way You did.
May I never use my anger to hurt someone.*

HURRY!

One who moves too hurriedly misses the way.
PROVERBS 19:2 NRSV

Hurry. Move faster. Accomplish more. Learn this. Study that. Do more. Fit more things into your life. Messages like these probably fly around you all the time. Many times the people who genuinely want the best for you are the ones who pressure you with these implied (or spoken) commands. But remember, you are following God. He will never tell you to hurry. He doesn't want you to dash through life and lose your way. Instead, He wants you to slow down a little so you can enjoy every minute of the wonderful life He's given you.

. . . .

When I feel like I have to go faster, faster, faster, Lord, remind me that it's never Your voice telling me to hurry. Teach me Your way, and help me to follow You.

DON'T WEAR OUT YOUR WELCOME!

When you find a friend, don't outwear your welcome;
show up at all hours and he'll soon get fed up.
PROVERBS 25:17 MSG

You want to be loved and accepted. Every young adult does (and so do older adults). It can be easy, though, to try too hard. You might cling too tightly to a boyfriend or expect your friends to *always* have time for you. Just as you need to have healthy boundaries, you also need to respect others' boundaries. That's part of following the Golden Rule: treat others the way you want them to treat you.

No friend can meet all your needs, and it's not fair to expect them to. Instead, rely on God. He never gets tired of hearing your voice. You can never wear out your welcome with Him!

. . . .

Show me, Father God, how to recognize
my friends' boundaries—and respect them.
Thank You that when I'm lonely, You are
always there to listen and be with me.

INSULTS

A wise person stays calm when insulted.
PROVERBS 12:16 NLT

No one likes to be criticized. It's not easy to stay calm when someone points out your faults or flaws. Sometimes we do need someone to show us things about ourselves we've been refusing to see, but that's different from the hurtful insults that get slung around your high school. People also tend to feel free to be more insulting on social media than they would be in person. It's only natural to get upset when you read something ugly about yourself online. But try to stay calm. Don't respond to the insults—or if you do, simply say you're not going to engage in a conversation that's disrespectful of who you are. Don't take the ugly words to heart; instead, ask for God's help and protection. Let the insults roll off you like water off a duck's back. And then forget them!

* *

Why are people so mean sometimes, Lord? Thank You that You are always right there, ready to protect me and keep me calm. I don't want to engage in this game of tossing insults back and forth, so remind me to respect myself enough to walk away.

OPEN YOUR ARMS AND YOUR HEART

*She opens her arms to the poor and
extends her hands to the needy.*

PROVERBS 31:20 NIV

Schoolwork, family chores, after-school activities, time with friends—all these things keep you busy. You may feel as though you have no time for anything else. But God wants you to remember that there are people who could use your help. You might volunteer through your church or school, or you could look online to see which charities in your area are looking for some help. Reaching out to those in need doesn't always have to be something organized and official, either. Lonely people are everywhere—not only in nursing homes and hospitals, but also in your own school and even in your family—and taking time to talk to them and listen can bring joy to their lives. Maybe someone just needs a hug. Ask God to show you where you could do good in the world today, this week. And then trust Him to help you make room in your busy schedule.

• •

*Show me where I'm needed, Lord God. Please open
my heart—and then use me to show others Your love.*

TROUBLE

The LORD is good, a refuge in times of trouble.
He cares for those who trust in him.

NAHUM 1:7 NIV

Coping with trouble isn't easy. You probably ask your-self, *Why did something bad have to come along and upset my life just when everything was going so well?* But if you take a few deep breaths, focusing on God, you may find that the situation isn't quite as bad as you'd thought. Now imagine yourself in a safe refuge—a hiding place—with God. Try focusing on something else, just for the next half hour. Even with this trouble in your life, you can still appreciate life's small pleasures: a beautiful sunrise, your dog's slobbery kisses, your friend's laughter. Think about those things instead of the big bad trouble that has just landed in your life. No matter how desperate you feel at times, God is still there, still blessing you in big and small ways.

Father God, I'm feeling pretty discouraged
and upset right now—but I know You are with
me. Remind me to keep my eyes open for all
the good things You've put in my life.

LiFE CYCLE

Happy are those who are kind to the poor.
PROVERBS 14:21 NRSV

We live in a world where everything is connected—tiny one-celled creatures, plants, animals, human beings, you, me. When we act selfishly, taking what we want while harming a part of this network of life, we ultimately end up harming ourselves. Our damaged environment is a good example of human selfishness that has hurt us all. Nearly three thousand years ago, the wise author of Proverbs already understood this principle. If we had all listened to him, the world might be in better shape today!

Remember: What's good for you is good for me, and what hurts you will end up hurting me too. When you are kind to others, that kindness will come back to you. That's the cycle God created for life.

. . . .

Remind me, Lord, not to be selfish. Teach me to focus more on giving generously and showing kindness than on trying to get what I want.

THE FUTURE

*"For I know the plans I have for you," declares
the L*ord*, "plans to prosper you and not to harm
you, plans to give you hope and a future."*

Jeremiah 29:11 niv

When you feel discouraged, this verse is a good one
to read. No matter how terrible things may seem right
now, God promises there is always something better
up ahead. He has a plan for your life—and it's a plan
you're going to love! God doesn't want you to spend
your entire life being sad or feeling like a failure. He
wants you to be happy; He wants you to love being
you; and most of all, He wants you to know how much
He loves you. You're important to Him, and your life
has an important purpose in His kingdom.

* *

*When I get discouraged, Lord God, remind me that
You hold my future in Your hands. Help me to trust
You. I want to serve my purpose in Your kingdom.*

LEARN AS MUCH AS YOU CAN!

Commit yourself to instruction;
listen carefully to words of knowledge.
PROVERBS 23:12 NLT

As a young woman, you have opportunities and freedoms women didn't have a hundred years ago. Women are no longer considered incapable of learning; everyone knows now that women are just as intelligent as men. This means you have so many more choices in life than your grandmother and great-grandmother had. You can explore and learn in all sorts of areas. The world is open to you, waiting for you to step into it and make a difference—so learn as much as you possibly can. Absorb as much as you can of the knowledge that's out there. You're already a wonderful young person, and you're going to be a wonderful adult too. So get ready. Study. Learn. God has big plans for you.

. . . .

Thank You, Father God, for the plans You have for my
life. Help me to do everything I can to learn and grow
so that I'm ready for whatever You have in mind.

BE DIRECT!

An open, face-to-face meeting results in peace.
PROVERBS 10:10 MSG

You might have learned that it's more loving to avoid honest communication than to share what you really feel, think, or need. That mentality has been taught to many women; and unfortunately, it's still around today. A lot of women just aren't comfortable with confrontation. But when we don't express our real feelings and needs, they often come out anyway—just "sideways" rather than directly. So instead of telling a friend why you feel upset with her, you gossip about her behind her back. Or you yell at your little sister when really you're angry with your boyfriend. That guy who wrote the book of Proverbs was pretty wise, though; he knew that being honest and direct is the best way to get along.

. . . .

Give me the courage I need, Lord, to speak out when I'm upset about something. Remind me that I don't need to be ashamed of having needs and feelings. Show me how to express myself clearly, kindly, and gently.

your words

Kind words heal and help;
cutting words wound and maim.
PROVERBS 15:4 MSG

Sticks and stones may break my bones, but words will never hurt me. People have been repeating that line for more than a hundred years. But is it true? Mental-health researchers have found that, in fact, words *do* hurt. Unkind teasing and verbal bullying can cause low self-esteem, depression, and even suicidal thoughts. Our words are powerful. But on the flip side, kind, encouraging words can heal and help. When everyone in your group of friends is making fun of someone, it can be so easy to go along—but God wants you to be careful to use your words to help others rather than wound them.

. . . .

Give me the strength, Lord God, to be kind, even when everyone around me is being mean. Teach me to speak words of help and healing, and forgive me for any words I've spoken that may have hurt someone. Show me how I can make amends.

ACCEPTING OTHERS' ADVICE

*Without good direction, people lose
their way; the more wise counsel you
follow, the better your chances.*
PROVERBS 11:14 MSG

Pretty much everyone has a GPS in their phones these days, so you may not have had much experience with being lost. In the "old days," though, before the GPS went mainstream, people depended on maps. When they got lost, they had to stop and ask for directions.

When it comes to life, you don't have a GPS to keep you on track. There's no little voice telling you where to turn or how far to go in a certain direction; there's no one to reroute you when you take a wrong turn. So if you feel as though you've gotten lost somehow—maybe in a relationship, in your schoolwork, or in a habit you know isn't healthy—it could be time to stop and "ask for directions." Talk to friends and adults you trust, and then ask God to help you choose the right path ahead.

. . . .

*Sometimes, Lord, I don't want to listen to anyone.
I just want to do things my way. Help me remember
that getting advice won't take away my independence,
but it could keep me from making a mistake!*

GOD LIKES YOU

A good person basks in the delight of God.
PROVERBS 12:2 MSG

Knowing that a friend enjoys being with you makes you feel good inside, doesn't it? We all like to know that the people we like, like us back. But have you ever felt that someone you know who loves you really doesn't *like* you? They don't like spending time with you. You feel like you get on their nerves. But that's not the way God feels about you. God not only loves you, He also likes you! In fact, He really, really likes you and enjoys your company. You make Him happy when you spend time with Him. You make Him laugh with delight!

*Father God, it's hard for me to grasp that
You like me. You seem too big and far away
sometimes. Remind me that You are always with
me. You are even inside of me. We can spend
time together every moment of every day.*

28

WHEN PLANS DON'T WORK OUT

*The human mind plans the way,
but the LORD directs the steps.*
PROVERBS 16:9 NRSV

Even when you make the most careful plans, things don't always turn out the way you imagined they would. Life is unpredictable. Circumstances—bad weather, illness, or a scheduling conflict, for example—can upset your plans. When that happens, you may feel disappointed, frustrated, maybe even infuriated. But God can use whatever happens. He can guide you through all the surprises and disappointments life throws at you. He can bring something even better than you imagined out of your shattered plans. He knows the way. He is the absolute best trail guide you could ever have.

When things don't go the way I planned, Lord, help me to trust You. Teach me to let go of my ideas about what should happen, and open my eyes to whatever wonderful thing You are doing in my life instead.

ANTS!

*Look at an ant. Watch it closely; let it teach you.
. . . Nobody has to tell it what to do. All summer it
stores up food; at harvest it stockpiles provisions.*

PROVERBS 6:6–8 MSG

Ants are interesting little creatures. They live in communities where each member does its job without complaining. No one has to yell at them or bribe them to get them to do their work. They never goof off or feel too lazy to show up.

Human beings are not ants, of course. You can't work all the time, like an ant does; it wouldn't be healthy for you, physically, emotionally, socially, or spiritually. Still, the world of nature—including ants—can teach you important things. Open your eyes and look at the world God created. What message might He be speaking to you through the plants, the trees, the insects, and all the other living creatures of the natural environment around you?

- -

*Thank You, Father God, for creating such an
interesting world. Teach me to respect it and learn
from it. I want to absorb whatever lessons You
want me to learn—even if they come from ants!*

BE DiSCERNiNG!

The discerning heart seeks knowledge.
PROVERBS 15:14 NIV

Being gullible is not the same as being open-minded. God wants you to be ready and willing to consider other perspectives besides your own, but He doesn't want you to let people take advantage of you. So don't let people manipulate you for their own purposes. Look past what they're saying and see if you can tell what their real motivation is. Don't take everything at face value, and don't let yourself be a target for others' abuse. Instead, set your boundaries and stand your ground. Believe in your own value, and don't let anyone take that away from you. Be discerning in your relationships.

. . . .

Lord God, I need Your wisdom so that I can see when people are trying to manipulate me. Show me if anyone is taking advantage of me. Help me to be strong and brave enough to stand up for myself.

BE CAREFUL WHAT YOU SAY!

*Watch your words and hold your tongue;
you'll save yourself a lot of grief.*

PROVERBS 21:23 MSG

Do you tend to say almost anything that pops into your mind? When you're talking and laughing with your friends, it can be really easy to do this. But then something slips out that you didn't mean to say. Maybe you betray a friend's confidence. Or you exaggerate so much that what you're saying really isn't true. Maybe you don't realize how your words sound, and without intending to, you hurt someone. This is why that wise man who wrote Proverbs tells us to be careful with our words. If you think before you speak, you can prevent a lot of pain both to others and to yourself.

. . . .

*When I'm having a good time with my friends, Lord,
remind me to be careful what I say. Help me to catch
myself before I say something unkind or untrue. Help
me to always use my words to spread Your love.*

YOU'RE BEAUTIFUL!

You are altogether beautiful,
my darling; there is no flaw in you.
SONG OF SONGS 4:7 NIV

Do you ever look in the mirror and not like what you see? Maybe you wish you were thinner. . .or had thicker hair. . .or a smaller nose. But God makes no mistakes—and He certainly didn't make a mistake when He made you! You are beautiful, unique, and just the way He wants you to be. In His eyes, you are absolutely perfect. Maybe you're thinking, *Well, that's nice that God thinks I'm perfect, but what I really want is for that cute boy in my class to like the way I look.* Those thoughts are normal, but try to remember that the approval of the Creator of the universe matters more than what any human thinks. And the next time you find yourself feeling discouraged when you look in the mirror, remind yourself: *God thinks I'm beautiful.*

Dear Father God, sometimes I really wish
I looked different. Help me to see myself
the way You see me. Help me not to care so
much about what other people think.

FAITH

*The fundamental fact of existence is that this
trust in God, this faith, is the firm foundation
under everything that makes life worth living.
It's our handle on what we can't see.*

HEBREWS 11:1 MSG

What is faith, anyway? Is it your religion? Is it the church
you attend? Or is it something personal and private?

Actually, your church or religion can help you build
your faith; those things can give you a foundation and
structure for your beliefs. But faith is something still
deeper; it has to do with letting go of your control of
your life. God wants you to enjoy the many wonderful
things He created, but He doesn't want you to cling
to them. Instead, faith puts everything in life back
into God's hands. Faith also allows you to look past
appearances; it believes that no matter what life may
look like, God is doing something amazing. Faith knows
that life is full of mystery, but it is confident that God's
love will never fail. And the more time you spend with
God, the greater your faith will be!

*Help my faith in You to grow, Lord. May it be
the foundation of my life and the "handle"
I use to look ahead to the future.*

TRUST AND DOUBT

Trust GOD from the bottom of your heart;
don't try to figure out everything on your own.
PROVERBS 3:5 MSG

Even the strongest Christians you know have doubts sometimes. Doubting isn't a sin. It's just part of the human experience. So when you have doubts about God, He doesn't get mad. And even when you are full of doubts, you can still trust God.

How do you do that? By going ahead with life, one step at a time, doing the things you know God wants—things like being kind, generous, truthful, and loving. Ultimately, doubt is just a feeling, an emotion, and your emotions come and go. Your actions can express your trust in God even when your emotions are wobbling. You make God happy when you show through your actions that you trust Him, and before you know it, you'll realize He's with you after all.

. . . .

I can't figure things out on my own, Lord, and
sometimes I'm scared You're just my imaginary
friend. I'm afraid You're not real, that no one
is there to listen when I pray. When I feel that
way, help me still to follow Your path of love. I
want to trust You even when I have doubts!

EQUALITY

The rich and the poor shake hands as
equals—GOD made them both!
PROVERBS 22:2 MSG

Regardless of skin color, gender, age, religion, financial status, or nationality, God loves everyone equally. He wants everyone to be treated fairly. People, however, keep forgetting this lesson that is everywhere in the Bible.

In Bible times, God got angry when rich people took advantage of poor people. He challenged His people to change their ways, and He showed them a better way to live. Today, we still need to learn this lesson. We need to look at our world and see where things aren't fair, and then we need to work to change things. We need to work with God to build a better world where everyone is safe, where all have equal opportunities, and where everyone is respected and valued.

. . . .

Father God, I want to help You tear down the
parts of our world that aren't fair, the parts that
put some people's health and happiness in danger.
Show me the actions I can take even now as a young
adult. Don't let me be content to sit back and do
nothing while so many people are suffering.

EVERYONE NEEDS ENCOURAGEMENT

The words of the godly encourage many.
PROVERBS 10:21 NLT

Everyone needs encouragement. Your best friend needs it. Your teachers need it. Your siblings need it. So do your parents. And so do the people who work in your school cafeteria, your next-door neighbors, that annoying kid who gets on your nerves, and that cute boy in your class. In fact, pretty much anyone you meet could use some encouragement.

Encouragement doesn't mean we tell people it's okay for them to do wrong things. Instead, it helps people be their best selves—the people God wants them to be. And it's not hard. Sometimes all it takes is a smile and a hello.

. . . .

Lord God, remind me today that everyone I meet needs encouragement. Please use me in whatever ways You want to help other people know You love them and are for them.

HOW TO BE A GOOD FRIEND

The person who shuns the bitter moments of friends will be an outsider at their celebrations.
PROVERBS 14:10 MSG

That Proverbs guy sure had a lot of good advice! And isn't it interesting that thousands of years later, we are still learning from his wisdom? His words still make sense, even for teenagers in the twenty-first century.

In this verse, that wise man is offering you some insight into how friendships work: if you're unwilling to share your friends' hard times, they're not going to want to share their good times with you either. You might get tired of hearing about a friend's problems; when you're in a good mood, you don't want to be dragged down by someone else's sadness. But God wants friends to share everything, both the good times and the bad. You may have insights your friend needs—or she may just need to know that someone loves her and understands.

. . . .

Help me, Lord, to be a good friend. Teach me to be sensitive, compassionate, and patient—even when I don't feel like being any of those things. I want to treat others with the same kindness You show me.

MORE RELATIONSHIP ADVICE

Singing cheerful songs to a person with a heavy heart is like taking someone's coat in cold weather or pouring vinegar in a wound.

PROVERBS 25:20 NLT

Have you ever noticed how uncomfortable it feels to be with someone who just broke up with her boyfriend or whose parents are going through a divorce? You want to help your friend cheer up, but that can be frustrating when she doesn't seem to listen to your encouragement. Well, here he is again, that guy who wrote most of the book of Proverbs, with more good relationship advice! What he's saying this time is that when a person is hurting, she doesn't need you to be all giggly and silly. That's not going to cheer her up. In fact, it's giving her the exact opposite of what she needs and hurting her even more in the process. What she really needs is someone who is willing to be with her in her pain. Who will listen. Who will accept her heartache and have compassion. Doing those things will go much further to ease her sadness than any silly joke!

· ·

Help me, Lord, to be a good friend who listens, who understands, who is willing to share my friends' pain.

DISCIPLINE

To learn, you must love discipline.
PROVERBS 12:1 NLT

You probably connect the word *discipline* with teachers who send misbehaving kids to the principal's office. Maybe you think of disapproving grade-school teachers who wouldn't let your class go out on the playground if you were too noisy. But what our friend, the author of Proverbs, is referring to here isn't scolding or punishment. Instead, he's talking about learning the best ways to truly enjoy life—and then practicing them. Discipline is about learning to take care of yourself physically, emotionally, and spiritually. It's also about learning how to get along with others. God wants your life to be full of joy. Discipline is the path to the wonderful life He wants for you.

. . . .

Help me, Father God, to be willing to learn what I need to know in order to live my life the way You want me to. Thank You that You bless me in so many ways.

DISCERNMENT

The wise in heart are called discerning,
and gracious words promote instruction.
PROVERBS 16:21 NIV

Discernment lets you see what is real and what is fake, what is right and what is wrong. It's the power to grasp what is true, even when things are confusing. It's also the ability to see beauty—in nature, in art, in music, and in other people. When you develop discernment, you can tell when conversations are empty or hurtful. You choose your own words carefully. You're able to see which activities will take you away from God and which ones will bring you closer to Him. When people are being phony, you can see right through them—and then you see the true God-given beauty that's hidden within them.

Discernment isn't something that develops overnight. It's usually something you need to grow into. In the meantime, you can ask God's Spirit to discern what's best for you. And the more time you spend with the Lord, the faster your own discernment ability will grow.

. . . .

Spirit, I ask for Your help today in discerning
what is right, what is beautiful, what is real.
I trust You, and I want to learn from You.

DON'T BE SCARED

*Jesus spoke to them at once. "Don't be afraid,"
he said. "Take courage! I am here!"*

MARK 6:50 NLT

Imagine you're one of Jesus' disciples out on the sea in
your fishing boat. The wind is blowing and the clouds
are thick, but through the gloom, you see the shape of
a man coming toward you—and he seems to be walking on top of the waves! You blink, squint, look again,
but the shape is still there, coming closer and closer.
You shiver in fear—but then you hear a familiar voice
calling to you. It's Jesus! At the very moment when
you and the other disciples are most afraid, you find
that Jesus is there. He climbs into the boat with you,
and the winds die down.

When you're feeling scared about something in
your life, when you're not sure what's coming toward
you, right at that moment Jesus is saying to you, "Don't
be scared. I'm here." He climbs right into the situation
with you—and suddenly, things look better. No matter
what comes next, He will be with you.

• •

*Thank You, Jesus, for being with me when I'm
scared. Thank You for sharing my troubles.*

BAD NEWS

*They will have no fear of bad news; their
hearts are steadfast, trusting in the Lord.*
Psalm 112:7 niv

It would be nice to think that this verse is promising that you'll never get bad news. Sadly, that's not true. Bad news comes to all of us at one time or another. What this verse *is* saying is this: you don't have to be scared of bad news. Whatever happens, God is with you. He has things to teach you, if you are willing to learn, and He has ways He wants to use you, even when hard things happen. Trust Him. He can handle whatever comes, and He can hold you steady. You don't need to worry.

. . . .

*Help me, Lord, not to worry about things that
haven't happened yet. I know that no matter
what happens in my life, You'll be there with
me. Teach me to trust You so much that I don't
feel scared even when bad news does come.*

WAiTiNG

*Wait for the L<small>ORD</small>; be strong and take
heart and wait for the L<small>ORD</small>.*
P<small>SALM</small> 27:14 <small>NIV</small>

It's hard to wait. Maybe you're waiting to find out if you passed your driver's test. Or you're waiting to see if you get into your first-choice college. Or you're waiting for your parents to say you're old enough to have new privileges. Whatever it is you're waiting for, you probably feel impatient sometimes. You might get discouraged. But remember, God has a plan for your life. He'll bring good things into your life at exactly the right time.

Long, long ago, the psalmist had these same feelings you do now. He reminded himself to "be strong and take heart," and then he turned the situation around. Instead of waiting for someone or something to give him what he wanted, he shifted his attention to the Lord. Now he was waiting only for God, and he knew God could be trusted to bless him.

. . . .

*When I'm waiting for something, Lord
God, teach me to give my impatience and
discouragement, my frustration and worry to
You. Show me how to wait for Your blessings.*

GOOD FRIENDS

Whoever walks with the wise becomes wise.

PROVERBS 13:20 NRSV

You probably have many different kinds of friends. Some of them you're really close to; you're comfortable sharing your secrets with them, and you would never tell their secrets to anyone else. Other friends aren't as close; you like them, but you don't really know them all that well (and you would never tell them anything private).

Friends aren't just fun to have; they also teach us and shape who we are. That's why it makes sense to choose your close friends carefully. You don't have to ignore the other people you're not as close to, and you can still have a good time with them. But spend the most time with friends you admire, friends who bring out the best in you.

* *

*Thank You for my friends, Lord. May I
learn from them, and may I be the sort
of person they can learn from too.*

GIFTS THAT CALM

*A quietly given gift soothes an irritable person;
a heartfelt present cools a hot temper.*
PROVERBS 21:14 MSG

When your little brother gets on your nerves, your knee-jerk reaction may be to snap at him. When a friend shoots an angry remark your direction, you may want to retaliate. When your mother is in a bad mood and gives you a hard time, it's easy to give her a hard time right back. In this verse, though, the author of Proverbs has advice for you: a sincere gift can calm things down. He doesn't mean, though, that every time someone in your life is feeling angry, you have to actually wrap up a present and give it to them. Instead, you can give your little brother the gift of patience. You can ask your angry friend what is bothering her—and then take time to listen. When your mom is in a bad mood, you might want to do something nice for her. These small gifts can make all the difference!

Father God, when the people in my life are angry, help me not to get angry too. Use me, please, to spread Your peace and love.

IT WORKS BOTH WAYS

A friend loves at all times.
PROVERBS 17:17 NRSV

That Proverbs guy sure knew a lot about friendships. It makes you wonder what he was like. (Solomon wrote most of the book of Proverbs, and you can read some stories about him in the book of 1 Kings. He may have been very wise, but you'll see that he also made plenty of mistakes in his life!) Anyway, the author of Proverbs is saying here that a real friend loves you without setting any conditions. You don't have to act a certain way or dress a certain way to get her approval. She's there for you when you're sad, listening to you share your hurt. She's always on your side. Being with her makes you feel good about yourself; you like the person you are when you're with her.

And, of course, it works both ways. Friendship is never a one-way street. You have to give back to your friend just as much as you receive.

- -

Thank You for my friends, Lord God.
Help me to be a good friend to them.

FEAR

I am so bewildered I cannot hear, so terrified I cannot see. My mind reels, horror overwhelms me.
ISAIAH 21:3–4 NASB

Fear is a normal and healthy reaction; it's how our bodies warn us of danger. By flooding our bodies with adrenaline, which makes our hearts beat faster and our breath come quicker, fear gets our bodies ready to either run away or take action. But sometimes there's nowhere to run and no action we can take. In times like that, fear can be destructive, eating at our stomachs, making us tense, distracting our minds from thinking clearly.

If you're in the middle of a time like that, remember—no matter how you feel, God is still there with you. He is still your refuge. He is big enough to hold all your fear and anxiety, and He will never leave you.

* *

When I feel sick to my stomach with anxiety about something, Lord, remind me that You are still there. When I can't seem to stop worrying, teach me to turn to You for strength.

DENiAL

You've cleaned up your lives by following the truth.
1 PETER 1:22 MSG

Have you ever heard someone say, "I just can't believe it"? Refusing to acknowledge that something is wrong is a normal way to cope with anything that puts your sense of control at risk. A short period of denial can be helpful because it gives you time to absorb a new reality at a pace that won't send you into a tailspin.

But don't linger in denial. Instead, move on and face the truth, no matter how painful or scary it may be. Remember, God is with you through good days and bad, and He is there in all truth—even the truth that's hard to face. As you accept life as it is—not as you wish it would be—you grow closer to God.

. . . .

Father God, help me to face the truth, even when it's hard. Thank You that You'll never leave me.

HEALING WHEN YOU'RE SICK

The LORD protects and preserves them—they
are counted among the blessed in the land—he
does not give them over to the desire of their
foes. The LORD sustains them on their sickbed
and restores them from their bed of illness.

PSALM 41:2–3 NIV

The Bible is full of stories about people who were physically healed by God. These stories tell us that God heals bodies. But the Bible always makes clear that, ultimately, healing is a spiritual thing. God may use a physical illness—big or little—as a time to teach you something new about Himself.

Whether it's a nasty head cold, stomach cramps, or a serious chronic disease like asthma or diabetes, being sick is never fun. God wants to share this time with you, though, and you can invite Him into your suffering by taking all that you're feeling to Him in prayer. So if you're sick, go ahead and pray for healing—but let God choose to heal you in whatever way He wants.

. . . .

Thank You, Father, that You are always with me, even
on the days when I'm so sick I never get out of my
pajamas. Please make me whole both physically and
spiritually. I know You always do what is best for me.

PEACE

You will experience God's peace, which exceeds anything we can understand. His peace will guard your hearts and minds as you live in Christ Jesus.

PHILIPPIANS 4:7 NLT

The Bible word that is translated "peace" is actually *shalom*. It's a word that is full of meanings that add to the way we usually understand peace. We might define peace as being the opposite of fighting, but the Bible's peace also meant wholeness, wellness, safety, contentment, rest, comfort, and ease. This is the sort of peace that God promises will guard your heart and mind.

Jesus said, "I have told you these things, so that in me you may have peace. In this world you will have trouble. But take heart! I have overcome the world" (John 16:33 NIV). You can trust Jesus to be the guardian of your life. No matter what's happening in the outside world, He can create "shalom" in your heart and mind.

. . . .

Jesus, when I'm in the middle of a tough time, please give me Your peace. No matter what happens, keep me whole and safe.

WHEN YOUR HEART BREAKS

He heals the brokenhearted and binds up their wounds.
PSALM 147:3 ESV

Sooner or later, life will break your heart. Unfortunately, that's just the way life is. A boy you love might choose to be with someone else. Your dog, who has been your friend since you were a toddler, dies. Someone you love gets a serious illness. Or things just don't turn out the way you'd hoped. When things like these happen, your sense of safety wobbles. You might think about yourself and life in a different way.

But God has promised to heal your broken heart. You might feel guilty letting others see your sadness and pain; but with God, you never need to pretend you're something you're not. You don't need to impress Him with your maturity and strength. Instead, you can come to Him honestly, admitting just how weak you're feeling. When you do, He can enter your life in new ways. He'll heal your wounded heart and make you strong.

. . . .

When life hurts, Lord, please stay close to me.

HOPE

*I pray that God, the source of hope, will fill you
completely with joy and peace because you trust
in him. Then you will overflow with confident
hope through the power of the Holy Spirit.*

ROMANS 15:13 NLT

The hope the Bible talks about doesn't mean you're
merely wishing for something good to happen. The
Bible's hope means putting your whole heart into
relying on God. It means keeping your eyes focused on
Him no matter what, waiting for Him to show Himself
to you. The Lord never disappoints people who wait for
His help, who keep looking for Him and never give up.
Sometimes, though, it takes courage to keep hoping.
There is so much in your life you don't understand, so
much that seems scary or sad. But God is there with
you. He will go with you each step of the way. Because
of Him, you can be at peace even when there seems
to be trouble in every direction you turn. He will give
you hope in every situation.

*Holy Spirit, sometimes life looks pretty hopeless.
Please teach me to put my hope in You.*

SCARS

He sent out his word and healed them,
snatching them from the door of death.
PSALM 107:20 NLT

Bad times can leave scars on your heart. Even things that happened when you were little can still haunt you. You might feel as though there's a piece of you with so many scars it's almost dead. Those scars may make it hard for you to trust people. They can make it hard for you to trust God too. But the Lord understands, and He never gets mad at you. He wants to help heal the scars on your heart. He might use a counselor or a close friend to help you heal; you can ask Him to show you the right person to talk to about your scarred heart. You can pray that He'll show you what you need to do to be healed. Your scars may never go away, but they won't hurt so much anymore. They won't keep you from living the full and wonderful life God wants you to have.

. . . .

Please, Father God, bring back to life everything
inside me that feels dead so that I can be a
stronger, happier, more confident person,
able to share Your love with the world.

BARGAINING WITH GOD

"Will not the Judge of all the earth do right?"
GENESIS 18:25 NIV

Have you ever prayed, "Dear God, if only You'll make this thing in my life go away, I'll do such and such. . ."? That's called bargaining. Psychologists talk about bargaining as a way we act sometimes when something sad or scary happens. It's a pretty normal human reaction. Even the great heroes of faith in the Bible sometimes tried to bargain with God.

Bargaining doesn't change reality, though. There's nothing you can give to God that will make Him decide to magically fix the hard things in your life. But God understands, and He listens. When you trust Him, you can feel comfortable telling Him absolutely anything. You can even get mad and yell at God (people in the Bible did it all the time!), but eventually you're going to see that God does everything right. Even when life is hard, He's at work inside you and all around you, helping you grow into a strong, beautiful, and compassionate woman.

. . . .

When everything seems wrong, Lord, help me to trust that You're still doing everything right.

HARD TIMES

*Consider it pure joy. . .whenever you face trials
of many kinds, because you know that the
testing of your faith produces perseverance.*

JAMES 1:2–3 NIV

Sometimes the Bible is hard to understand. Why on earth would God want us to think that hard times are happy times? That just doesn't make sense! But what this Bible verse is really saying is this: when hard times and challenges come your way, don't let them get you down. The times when you're under pressure are the times when you grow the most. So let God do whatever He wants in your life, and He will help you feel happy even when times are tough. In the middle of the biggest messes, God will still bless you. That's why you can have joy—because nothing ever keeps God from loving you and working to make you the best "you" that you can be.

. . . .

*I still don't understand, Lord, why You think I
should be happy about trouble, but I know You
love me. Teach me whatever I need to learn.*

GOD'S LOVE

Love never gives up. . . . Always looks for the best, never looks back, but keeps going to the end. Love never dies.
1 CORINTHIANS 13:4–8 MSG

People often read these words at weddings because they describe what real love looks like. These verses can teach us how we should act and think when we love someone, but they also describe the way God loves you.

God never gives up on you.

God looks past your flaws and sees what is best in you.

God doesn't worry about what you did in the past; He's always focused on the person you are now and the person you are growing into.

God's love never wears out. It never goes away. The Creator of the universe loves *you*, no matter what, forever and ever.

. . . .

It's hard to believe, Father God, that You love me so much. Please keep teaching me; keep showing me Your love.

SAY YES TO LIFE!

"I came so they can have real and eternal life,
more and better life than they ever dreamed of."
JOHN 10:10 MSG

Have you ever thought that people who call themselves Christians seem to live boring lives? Or have you thought that following Jesus means saying no to so many things that it's hard to have any fun? It's easy to get that impression from some people, but that's not the kind of life Jesus was talking about in this verse. Jesus came to earth in a human body and died on the cross so you could have the best life possible, a life filled to the brim with wonderful things. Whenever Jesus asks you to say no to something, it's always because He wants you to say yes to something even better. The life He wants to give you is bursting with blessing upon blessing!

. . . .

Thank You, Jesus, that You loved me so much
You became a person like me. Thank You for the
wonderful life You give me. Please equip me with
the courage and strength to say no to anything
that might keep me from living close to You.

FRIENDS WITH GOD

*Long enough, GOD. . . . Long enough I've carried this
ton of trouble, lived with a stomach full of pain.
Long enough my arrogant enemies have looked down
their noses at me. . . . I've thrown myself headlong
into your arms—I'm celebrating your rescue.*

PSALM 13:1–2, 5 MSG

This psalm seems all over the place, doesn't it? Like
most of the book of Psalms, it was written by a man
named David. The psalms written by David are prayers
that he wrote as though he were talking directly to
God. If you read through the book of Psalms, you'll
see that David didn't just worship and praise God;
he also complained to Him! He was honest with God
about whatever he was feeling, and he even admitted
to being angry with the Lord. Whatever David was
feeling, he brought it to God. He talked to God about
absolutely everything. Even when he was mad at God,
he still trusted Him. And even when David messed up
(which he did), he still knew God loved him and would
forgive him.

. . . .

*Teach me, Lord God, how to be more like David in the
Bible. I want to be friends with You the way he was.*

BEING HONEST WITH GOD

Wake up, O Lord! Why do you sleep? Get up!
Do not reject us forever. Why do you look the
other way? Why do you ignore our suffering
and oppression? . . . Rise up! Help us!
PSALM 44:23–24, 26 NLT

Most Christians today don't talk much about being angry with God. You don't often see people stand up in church and say, "I'm so mad at God right now!" Instead, people act as though their faith is so great that it takes away their normal human reactions to hard things. If you ever find yourself feeling angry with God about something, you may think you need to pretend your anger isn't there. You might feel guilty admitting it out loud to anyone.

But here again, David, the author of many psalms, had no problem telling God how he felt. So go ahead—be honest with God about your feelings. But also be confident that He hears you, He doesn't get mad at you, and He will come to help you.

. . . .

Thank You, Father God, that I can tell You everything.
Teach me to trust You the way David did.

BECAUSE OF JESUS

"This is how much God loved the world: He gave
his Son, his one and only Son. And this is why:
so that no one need be destroyed; by believing in
him, anyone can have a whole and lasting life."

JOHN 3:16 MSG

If you grew up going to Sunday school, you might have learned this verse by heart. The words might be so familiar that you don't really hear them anymore. You might not stop to consider what they're saying. So take a moment now to think about what this verse really means. It's the message Jesus brought to us, wrapped up in a neat summary:

God loves you.

God gives you His Son, Jesus.

Because of Jesus, you can have a wonderful life right now.

Because of Jesus, you can live forever, even after you die.

. . . .

Thank You, Jesus, for showing me God's love.

MORE THAN YOU CAN ASK OR THINK

*God. . .is able, through his mighty power
at work within us, to accomplish infinitely
more than we might ask or think.*

EPHESIANS 3:20 NLT

"More than we might ask or think"—that's a pretty amazing description of what God wants to do for you. Imagine every good thing you've ever dreamed about. Think of things too wonderful to ever be true. And you still won't have reached the limit of what God wants for you.

This doesn't mean, of course, that one day you'll fly through the sky on the back of your very own flying unicorn (although who knows what heaven will be like?). And it doesn't mean that God is like a magic genie who will give you all your wishes. But it *does* mean He's going to do incredible things in your life. When you give your life to God, the new life He gives you ends up being better than you ever imagined. There are no limits to what God can do.

. . . .

*Thank You, Lord God, for all the awesome
things You are doing in my life.*

REJECTED

*"Those the Father has given me will come
to me, and I will never reject them."*

JOHN 6:37 NLT

Have you ever felt rejected by someone? Maybe the
"popular group" refused to be friends with you. A boy
you liked might have chosen someone else to be his
girlfriend. You didn't get picked to be in the school
play, or your friend invited someone else to go to a
concert with her instead of you. Sometimes, when
you feel as though your parents are always criticizing
you, you might even feel that they've rejected you,
that they don't accept the real you.

But Jesus said that He will never reject you. When
you come to Him, He always has time for you, He always
pays attention, and He never criticizes you. He is the
best friend you could ever have!

*When I feel sad because someone has rejected me,
Lord Jesus, remind me that You always accept me just
the way I am. You always love me no matter what.*

WHATEVER GOD WANTS

"I can do nothing on my own. . . . I seek to do not my own will but the will of him who sent me."

JOHN 5:30 NRSV

God wants to give you absolutely everything—but He also wants you to give absolutely everything back to Him. This means you accept whatever God sends into your life. But it *doesn't* mean you lie down like a doormat for the world to walk over. You might need to work to change the things happening around you; maybe you need to take a stand and say, "This is wrong!" But first, you accept the situation. You don't stomp your feet and say, "It's not fair that I have to go through this!" Instead, you say, "Thank You, Lord, for this situation—and thank You for the way You will show Yourself to me through this situation. Show me how to respond to what's happening. Is there something I could do to make things better? Let me know if and when I should take action. I want to do whatever You want."

. . . .

Lord Jesus, help me to follow Your example by giving everything back to Your Father.

SPIRIT FRUIT

*But the fruit of the Spirit is love, joy, peace, patience,
kindness, goodness, faithfulness, gentleness,
self-control; against such things there is no law.
Now those who belong to Christ Jesus crucified
the flesh with its passions and desires. If we live
by the Spirit, let's follow the Spirit as well.*
GALATIANS 5:22–25 NASB

When the Bible refers to all these good qualities—love,
joy, peace, patience, and so on—it calls them "fruit of
the Spirit." In other words, when the Spirit of God lives
within you, His presence will just naturally show up in
the way you feel and talk and act. You don't have to
pretend to be better than you really are, and you don't
have to work really hard to make these good qualities
appear in your life. Instead, as you focus more and
more on God, He will take care of the rest of it. Like
an apple tree with its apples or an orange tree with
oranges, your life will be sweet with the Spirit's fruit.

*Jesus, help me to grow closer and closer
to You. Show me how to make more and
more room in my life for the Spirit.*

DEATH

*"Trust me. There is plenty of room for you in my
Father's home. If that weren't so, would I have told
you that I'm on my way to get a room ready for
you? And if I'm on my way to get your room ready,
I'll come back and get you so you can live where I live."*

JOHN 14:1–3 MSG

Do you ever think about death? Death is the great
mystery; no one (except Jesus) gets to come back
and tell us what things are like on the other side of
death. When we think about death, most of us feel sad
or scared. We don't like to think about the people we
love dying, and we sure don't like to think about dying
ourselves! But we don't have to be afraid of death. Yes,
when a person we love dies, we'll feel sad—but we can
be confident that death is not the end. We know that
because Jesus told us! He understands that death is
sad (He cried when His friend Lazarus died), but He
doesn't want us to fear death anymore. If we have put
our trust in Him, He has a wonderful space in heaven
prepared just for us.

. . . .

*Thank You, Jesus, for letting me know that You
have a special place for me in heaven. And thank
You for telling us the truth about death.*

WRAPPED IN GOD'S LOVE

*"But You are a God of forgiveness, gracious and
compassionate, slow to anger and abounding
in mercy; and You did not abandon them."*

NEHEMIAH 9:17 NASB

God invites you to come to Him with each day's events.
You can tell Him about the good things that happen,
and you can tell Him about the things that make you
feel sad or scared. He never threatens you or thinks
less of you, even if you forget to talk to Him for days
in a row. Instead He waits and promises to listen to
whatever you want to tell Him. He wants to calm you
when you're anxious, comfort you when you're sad,
and laugh with you when you're happy. If you have a
bully who lives inside your mind, constantly criticizing
you and predicting that you're going to mess up, God
wants to hush that bully up. God wants to wrap you
up in His love.

*Thank You, Lord God, that You are such a good
friend, always there, always ready to listen and
help. Thank You for loving me so much.*

LIVING WITH GOD

*GOD's blessing makes life rich; nothing
we do can improve on God.*

PROVERBS 10:22 MSG

In a world where everything is constantly changing, God is always the same, yet never boring. He's always loving, creative, kind, compassionate, and understanding. He protects, loves, and guides you. Every morning He's right beside you. He never walks out when you're talking to Him. Just think of this: God rules the universe; He knows about each star in our galaxy, and He's familiar with all the galaxies outside our own. And this same God is concerned with you and your life. His presence fills the vast reaches of space, and He lives inside your heart. Living with Him, loving Him, you'll find your life to be rich with happiness, adventure, and fun.

. . . .

*You bless me in so many ways, Father God.
You are amazing. I want to live with You forever.*

GOOD NEWS

In your hearts revere Christ as Lord. Always be prepared to give an answer to everyone who asks you to give the reason for the hope that you have. But do this with gentleness and respect.

1 PETER 3:15 NIV

The word *gospel* means "good news," and the message of Jesus is such good news that you should want to share it with others. God loves us! That is the best news ever. But that doesn't mean you should clobber people over the head with your beliefs. Instead, the Bible advises that you go about your life with joyful hope, living for Jesus, learning from His Spirit, and growing in God. Then when people notice there's something different about you and the way you live, you can be ready to answer their questions. Even then, God wants you to honor the other person and her beliefs. You don't make fun or criticize but instead speak gently, with genuine love and respect.

. . . .

Jesus, I want Your love to shine out of me so that others will see You in my life. Help me to be comfortable talking about You when people ask me about You.

COMPLAINING

I pour out my complaints before him
and tell him all my troubles.

PSALM 142:2 NLT

When you're upset about something, don't feel guilty if you find yourself asking God over and over why He allowed things to happen this way. Complaining to God doesn't make you less of a Christian. So long as you're sharing your true feelings with God, complaining won't interfere with your relationship with Him. Even Jesus experienced feelings of frustration and distress. On the cross, He asked His Father, "Why? Why did You abandon Me?" (see Matthew 27:46). Like Jesus, you too might feel sometimes as though God has forgotten about you. But in the Bible, God says to you, "Can a mother forget her baby? Even if a mother could forget her baby, I will never forget you!" (see Isaiah 49:15). You're safe with God—safe enough to complain, safe enough to know He'll never leave you.

* *

Father God, I don't understand why You let
some things happen. I don't want to doubt Your
goodness, though. Help me to trust You more.
Thank You that I can tell You anything.

A BIG LIFE

May the LORD cause you to flourish.
PSALM 115:14 NIV

You've probably heard Christians talk quite a bit about the eternal life Jesus gives. A lot of times, people talk as though that life is something we won't get to experience until after we die, when we get to heaven. But really, eternal life begins right now. When you give your life to Jesus, He makes your life fuller, wider, deeper. He gives you *more* life than you ever knew was possible. Some Bible versions translate the word *flourish* in this verse as *increase*; in other words, God will make your life BIGGER. He'll help you grow in all sorts of ways, and He'll bring exciting new experiences into your life. With Him, you'll *never* stop growing!

. . . .

Jesus, I want to live my life with You. Thank You for the amazing life You give me. Teach me to trust You more and more, believing that You want to help me grow.

GOD'S GIFTS

*Every good and perfect gift is from above, coming
down from the Father of the heavenly lights.*

JAMES 1:17 NIV

Have you ever gotten the impression that pretty much anything you enjoy is a temptation to sin? Some adult followers of Jesus may act that way. (They may even believe it, which is pretty sad.) It's true that anything that's more important to you than God can be a problem. Whether it's a relationship with a friend or boyfriend, a sport you love, a talent you have, or even just a preoccupation with video games, if it comes between you and God, it can keep your relationship with Him from growing. But that doesn't mean the things you like most are sins in and of themselves. All the good things in your life come directly from God. They're a part of the life He has blessed you with right now, and He loves seeing you enjoy His gifts.

. . . .

*I'm so grateful, Lord God, for all the wonderful
things You've given me. Help me never to make
them more important to me than You are.*

ETERNAL LOVE

*"I have loved you, my people, with an everlasting love.
With unfailing love I have drawn you to myself."*

JEREMIAH 31:3 NLT

God's love never ends. It never fails. It's unconditional.
It's bigger and deeper than anything you could ever
comprehend, because it has no limits, no boundary lines
it refuses to cross. Wherever you go, it follows you. It
pulls you closer to God. It never fades away; it never
dies; it will never fail you. People talk about "eternity"
as though it's the same thing as "heaven"—but really,
eternity is the love of God. It's here right now, it was
there yesterday, and it will still be there tomorrow.
God's love is the life that never ends, and His love
gives that life to you.

. . . .

*I keep learning more and more about Your love,
Lord, and the more I learn, the more wonderful I
realize You are! Help me to never stop learning.
Please fill me forever with Your love.*

BLESSINGS

*"I'm going to show them life whole,
life brimming with blessings."*
JEREMIAH 33:6 MSG

The Lord showers you with so many good things each day—your family, your friends, your school, your body with all its abilities, your talents, and the beautiful planet on which you live. Some days, though, these gifts may not seem all that nice; your family gets on your nerves, your friends hurt your feelings, you're bored with school, you don't like your body, and your talents don't seem to measure up to other people's. Sometimes it's easy to focus on all the negatives rather than the positives in life. "Counting your blessings" can seem kind of silly, but the more attention you give to everything that's good in your life, the less the not-so-good things will bother you.

. . . .

Teach me, Lord God, to spend more time thinking about all the good things You've given me and less time thinking about all the things that bug me.

SPIRIT POWER

The Spirit of God, who raised Jesus from the dead,
lives in you. And just as God raised Christ Jesus
from the dead, he will give life to your mortal
bodies by this same Spirit living within you.

ROMANS 8:11 NLT

Change can be both exciting and scary. Changing a
habit or moving outside your comfort zone can make
you feel anxious and out of control. Moving to a new
school, getting ready to go to college, or starting a new
job can be an exciting adventure but also can make you
feel worried and nervous. Remember, though, that the
same power of God that formed the universe at the
very beginning of time, that shaped our planet with all
its beauty and variety, and that raised Jesus from the
dead is alive and active today. And this same power is
at work in your life. The Spirit lives inside you, and the
Spirit is always available to help you work out the details
of your life. God will never leave you on your own.

Spirit of God, remind me that Your power is at
work in my life, both inside me and in everything
that happens to me and around me. Teach me to
turn to You whenever I feel worried or scared.

WALKING ON WATER

"I do believe; help me overcome my unbelief!"
MARK 9:24 NIV

Peter was walking along on the surface of the water, his eyes fixed on Jesus, doing just fine. Suddenly, he realized what he was doing. He looked at the waves beneath his feet, and he knew that what he was doing was *impossible*. Instantly, his feet sank into the water. He knew he was going to drown. But Jesus didn't let him. He grabbed His good friend and saved him.

And He will do the same for you. Doubts will keep popping up, though. You'll probably always have them. Over and over, every time you're swamped with doubts and start to sink, Jesus will reach out His hand to you. "Why do you doubt Me?" He'll ask each time. "Have I *ever* let you sink?"

• •

Thank You, Jesus, that You never let me drown.
No matter how many times I doubt You,
You always reach out and save me one more time.

PRAYER AND ALONE TIME

Jesus often withdrew to lonely places and prayed.

LUKE 5:16 NIV

Jesus is your perfect role model. In other words, He's the best person for you to imitate, so if He went away sometimes to be alone and pray, you should too. No one can be strong and healthy if they never take time for themselves. And no relationship can grow if you don't spend time sharing yourself. That's why spending time alone and in prayer is so important. You can pray while you shower, while you ride the bus to school, or while you lie in bed before you fall asleep—but it's also good to set aside a specific time (and even a specific place) for prayer. You can start slow: spend just five minutes every day alone (in your bedroom or in a favorite place outdoors) with God. As this becomes a habit, you may find you want to spend more and more time alone with God, just as Jesus did.

. . . .

Jesus, I'm so glad You came to earth to be our role model. Help me to imitate You. Help me to love like You—and pray like You.

THE EYES OF YOUR HEART

*I pray that the eyes of your heart may be
enlightened in order that you may know the
hope to which he has called you, the riches of his
glorious inheritance in his holy people, and his
incomparably great power for us who believe.*

EPHESIANS 1:18–19 NIV

You may wonder what this verse means when it talks about "the eyes of your heart." When the Bible talks about "heart," it doesn't mean the organ in your chest that pumps your blood. Instead, the word *heart* in the Bible refers to your inner self, the center of your being—the part of you that thinks and feels. So when the eyes of your heart open to God's light, you see things more clearly. You begin to understand God better, and you notice all the ways He's at work in your life. You begin to see from God's perspective instead of a human perspective. And that means you see with the eyes of love.

*Open my inner eyes, Father God, so I can see
You more clearly, and help me to see others
around me the way You see them too.*

GOD LISTENS!

I love the LORD because he hears my voice.
PSALM 116:1 NLT

Remember how we said earlier that David was the author of most of the psalms in the Bible? David lived about three thousand years ago. He messed up many times, but he and God never stopped being friends. Today, thousands of years after David's time on earth, you still might see a lot of yourself in David, and you can learn from him too. David went through times when he felt lonely, when no one around him seemed to understand him or wanted to listen to his feelings. That's why David was such good friends with God— because he knew God was always ready to listen. You can have the same kind of relationship with God that David had. God is always ready to listen to you. He always understands. The Creator of the universe, the one who made every atom, every particle, every star and planet in existence, hears *your* voice.

. . . .

I want to be friends with You, Lord God, the way David was. I know that friends need to talk to each other, so please remind me to keep talking to You. Thank You for always listening.

FOLLOWING GOD'S PATH

Blessed is the one. . .whose delight is in the law of the Lord. . . . That person is like a tree planted by streams of water, which yields its fruit in season and whose leaf does not wither.

PSALM 1:1–3 NIV

When the Bible talks about the "law of the Lord," it doesn't mean a bunch of rules and regulations. Instead, if you follow God's law, you stay on the path that leads to life and love. You make healthy decisions for yourself; your choices don't hurt yourself or others; you listen for God's direction and follow it. When you do that, you grow strong. God's life flows into you the way trees pull water up from the earth into their branches and leaves. Even when hard times come (and they always do, sooner or later), you will keep on growing. God will use your life to do good things in the world.

. . . .

I want to follow Your path, Lord. Help me to know what You want for my life.

HARD TIMES

*Have no fear of sudden disaster or of the ruin that overtakes the wicked, for the L*ORD *will be at your side and will keep your foot from being snared.*
PROVERBS 3:25–26 NIV

Bad things happen to both bad people and good people, of course. But when bad things happen to people who are following Jesus, who have given themselves to God, then God holds them even in the middle of trouble. He keeps them from falling flat on their faces. He uses even hard times to teach them new things and to help them grow. So don't worry about any trouble that may come your way. You can trust God to take care of you, no matter what happens. He won't let trouble trap you.

* *

When I feel worried or scared about all the bad things that can happen in life, remind me, Lord, that You are always with me. Even when trouble comes, Your love will keep me safe. You won't let me be trapped in something I can't handle.

GOD'S BiG PLANS

"No eye has seen, no ear has heard, and no mind has imagined what God has prepared for those who love him."

1 CORINTHIANS 2:9 NLT

God's promise for your future is so stupendous that you can't really understand it. He has great plans for you, and most of the time, you probably can't wait to find out what those plans are. You look forward to the future and all it holds. Other times, though, you may feel scared when you think about the future. You may even wish you could return to the past, to a time when you felt happy and safe. The future can seem frightening because it's uncertain; you can't know exactly what it will look like. While God doesn't give you a map that spells out exactly what direction your future will take, He does promise that it will be more than you could ever ask or imagine. He has big plans for you!

. . . .

Thank You, Father God, for all that lies ahead. Thank You for keeping me safe in the past, thank You for being with me now, and thank You that You'll stay with me every step of the way as I move into the future.

SMILE!

*"I will forget my complaint, I will change
my expression, and smile."*
JOB 9:27 NIV

Some days just don't go the way you planned. That can be frustrating. It might even make you mad. It's hard to accept that you don't have control over all the details of your life. What you *can* control, though, is your attitude. Although you can't instantly stop feeling upset, you can make the choice to smile. You can choose not to have a grouchy resting face! Scientists have discovered that smiling actually tricks your brain into being happy because all those tiny muscles that make a smile also trigger the release of brain chemicals that fight fear and sadness. So the next time you're feeling frustrated and angry, try focusing less on complaining—and more on smiling!

*Lord God, remind me to smile more and frown
less. May the expression on my face reflect
the presence of Your Spirit in my heart.*

THE KEYS TO GOD'S TREASURE HOUSE

*From his abundance we have all received
one gracious blessing after another.*

JOHN 1:16 NLT

God can give you so many good things because He Himself is overflowing with goodness. When you enter into a relationship with Him, He gives you access to all that goodness. It's kind of like being adopted by a king who gives you the keys to his treasure house and says, "All of my treasure belongs to you now. Go ahead and explore what I have. Help yourself to whatever looks good to you." As you get to know God better and better, you'll become aware that you live in a stream of God's blessing that never ends. All through your life—and even beyond death into the life that never ends—God's good gifts will never stop pouring out from His love.

. . . .

*Thank You, Father, for all the good things
You keep giving me. I'm so grateful You've
given me the keys to Your treasure house.*

THE BIBLE

Fix these words of mine in your hearts and minds; tie them as symbols on your hands and bind them on your foreheads.

DEUTERONOMY 11:18 NIV

Memorizing Bible verses isn't as big a thing as it used to be. Once upon a time (not that long ago), young people were expected to learn Bible verses as part of Sunday school classes and youth meetings, but nowadays not so much. Memorizing scripture in and of itself isn't all that important, of course—at least compared to loving God and others. Even if you memorized the entire Bible, that wouldn't necessarily make you a better person or prove that you know God—but learning certain important verses can give you a resource you'll be grateful for later in your life. You can draw strength and comfort in hard times from remembering what God said in the Bible. When you remember God's promises of love and hope, you'll have a source of strength you can turn to whenever you need it. As you hide portions of God's Word in your heart, they will help shape your thoughts and actions into a clearer reflection of God's love.

Even if I have trouble remembering Bible verses word for word, Lord, please remind me of Your promises whenever I'm in trouble. May I find comfort and strength in Your Word.

THE BODY OF CHRIST

You were all called to travel on the same road and in the same direction, so stay together, both outwardly and inwardly. . . . Everything you are and think and do is permeated with Oneness.
EPHESIANS 4:4, 6 MSG

If you're going through a hard time, everyone who loves you will be worried and upset too; likewise, if someone you love is sick or in trouble, you'll feel concerned as well. But when you pray for each other, you give your fears to God and help each other to be strong.

The "body of Christ" is a term the Bible uses to describe the oneness that believers have in Him; it also refers to the fact that together we represent Jesus and do His work on earth. Relationships—friendships and loving families—are what give the body of Christ strength and life. You experience the presence of Jesus through the love of your friends and family, and you in turn can show Jesus' love to them. You pray for each other and help each other face the hard things in life. You're better together than you would be alone.

. . . .

Thank You, Father God, for the people who love me, as well as the people I love. Help me to show them You through my words and actions, and teach me to see You in them. Show us how to lift each other up instead of drag each other down.

MEMORIES

For you have been my hope, Sovereign
LORD, my confidence since my youth.
PSALM 71:5 NIV

David, the author of this psalm, probably wrote these words during a time when he was going through some hard things. Earlier in the psalm, he described the disappointments and setbacks in his life, but in this verse, he remembers that God has been with him ever since he was young. By remembering what God did for him in the past, David gains courage for his current situation.

You can do the same thing. When you're in the middle of a tough time, think back to another time when you were in trouble. Remember how God got you through that time. Think about what you learned. Those memories can comfort you and make you stronger now. They can help you trust God to be with you in this present problem just as He was with you in the past.

When I'm in trouble, Lord, remind me of all
the ways You've helped me in the past.

REFUGE

*Trust in him at all times. Pour out your
heart to him, for God is our refuge.*

PSALM 62:8 NLT

In this psalm, David is talking to you from across three-hundred-some centuries, encouraging you to trust God all the time and to tell Him everything that is on your mind. Of course God already knows everything you think or feel, but He longs for you to come to Him, spilling out all your thoughts, even the silly ones. As you build a relationship with God like the one David had with Him, God will become the "place" you run to whenever you're feeling scared or sad or upset. That's what a "refuge" is: it's a place where you know you're safe, where no danger can reach you. That's what God was for David all those thousands of years ago, and that's what He wants to be for you today.

* *

*I want to learn to trust You more, Father God,
and I know that the closer I get to You, the
easier it will be for me to believe Your promises.
Remind me to run to You with all my worries.*

IN THE MORNING

*In the morning, Lord, you hear my voice; in the morning
I lay my requests before you and wait expectantly.*

PSALM 5:3 NIV

David, the author of this psalm, understood that his
relationship with God depended on being in constant
communication with Him. So David started each day
by talking over with God his concerns about the day
ahead. He let God know his plans for the day as well
as his worries and fears. But notice what David says
next: he *waits expectantly* for God. In other words, he
gives the day ahead to God, and then he steps back
to see what God will do. David doesn't insist that God
do exactly what he wants. Instead, he trusts that even
if his own plans fall through, God will do something
even better.

* *

*I'd like to start beginning each day with You,
Lord. Remind me to talk to You tomorrow
morning as I'm getting ready for the day.
Help me to trust You to take care of everything.*

A NEW DAY

You're our only hope. First thing in the morning,
be there for us! When things go bad, help us out!
ISAIAH 33:2 MSG

Every day is a new day, a new beginning, a new chance to enjoy your life because each day is a new gift from God. Each day offers new opportunities to be excited about all the things He's given you, to get to know Him better, and to find ways to spread His love to others. No matter what happened yesterday, when each morning comes, God gives you a fresh start, a fresh chance to have a closer relationship with Him. Whatever happens during this new day, He'll be there for you, ready to help—and He'll still be there at the end of the day. Spending time with God is a good way both to start your day and to end your day. Leave a little time before bedtime to connect with your heavenly Father, catching Him up on all the day's happenings.

Thank You, Father, that You were with me
yesterday, that You'll be with me today,
and that You'll still be with me tomorrow.

GOD LOVES YOU!

*"The L*ORD* your God is in your midst, a mighty one who will save; he will rejoice over you with gladness; he will quiet you by his love; he will exult over you with loud singing."*

ZEPHANIAH 3:17 ESV

Zephaniah, the man who wrote this verse, lived about three thousand years ago. He was a prophet. The Bible's prophets were people who were so close to God that He gave them messages to pass along to His people. Some of these messages were intended for particular situations that happened thousands of years ago, but many of them also have meaning for us today. Zephaniah's messages offer both comfort and challenge. He called for people to practice justice and turn to God, but he also reassured them of God's love.

Today, God sends you the same message Zephaniah wrote so long ago. "I am with you," God says to you. "I will rescue you whenever you're in trouble. You make Me happy. Let Me calm your worried heart with My love. I love you so much that I burst into song!"

. . . .

Thank You, Lord God, for Your love.

PARTNERS WITH JESUS

Be very glad—for these trials make you
partners with Christ in his suffering.
1 PETER 4:13 NLT

Jesus was a human being just like you are. He experienced the entire range of human emotions. He knew how it felt to be worried and lonely and sad. He didn't hold Himself separate from human experience; He shared it all, even death. This means that Jesus understands what you feel when you're hurting emotionally or physically. You can turn to Him, knowing that even if no one else understands what you're going through, He does. When you go through hard times, you can also come to know Jesus better. You and He can become partners in a new way.

. . . .

Help me, Lord Jesus, to share my life with You, both the
good times and the bad. I want to be partners with You
so that everything I do and say, I do and say with You.

GOD USES FRIENDS

The heartfelt counsel of a friend is as
sweet as perfume and incense.
PROVERBS 27:9 NLT

Whether you're talking face-to-face in the cafeteria, texting on your phones, or sharing pictures on social media, a true friend can help you know God better in all sorts of ways. No human friend is perfect, of course; we all let each other down sometimes, even when we don't mean to. But God can use your friends to show you His love. He uses their understanding and support to encourage you and their smiles and laughter to cheer you up. Your friends' insights can help you see things more clearly. As you share your lives with each other, God is present with you.

. . . .

Thank You for my friends, Lord. Help me to be a good friend, someone my friends can count on to listen and understand, someone who will stand with them in trouble and be at their side when they're sad. May my friends see You more clearly through our friendship.

GOD'S HELP

I lift up my eyes to the mountains—where does my help come from? My help comes from the LORD, the Maker of heaven and earth.

PSALM 121:1–2 NIV

As a teenager, you probably have more opportunities to make decisions for yourself than you did when you were younger. As you get older, you'll encounter more and more situations where you'll have the freedom to make your own choices. That's exciting. It can also be a little scary. What if you make the wrong choice? What if you make a mistake that messes up everything? We all have those fears, but you don't need to waste time worrying about them. As long as you keep your eyes on God, relying on Him for help, He'll make sure you stay on the right path. When you mess up—and you will, because everyone does!—God will find ways to use even your mistakes to teach you and help you grow.

. . . .

Lord God, as I get older and no longer need my parents to make all my decisions, I want to depend on You to help me and guide me.

SET FREE FROM FEAR

*The Spirit you received does not make you slaves,
so that you live in fear again; rather, the Spirit
you received brought about your adoption to
sonship. And by him we cry, "Abba, Father."*

ROMANS 8:15 NIV

Some people try to serve God because they're afraid
of Him. They don't want Him to send them to hell. But
that's not the kind of relationship God wants to have
with you. Instead, He wants you to experience the
freedom that comes from knowing you are loved. Fear
can make you its slave; it can keep you from doing the
things you'd like to do, the things God would like you to
do. Fear can also get in the way of enjoying life. It can
hold you back from new friendships, new experiences,
and new adventures. It can convince you to hide from
life rather than venture out with joy and confidence.

Jesus wants to set you free from fear.

*Thank You that I don't have to be afraid of You,
Jesus. Thank You that Your love sets me free.*

YOU'RE ON GOD'S MIND

What are mere mortals that you should think about them, human beings that you should care for them?

PSALM 8:4 NLT

Have you ever wondered what God thinks about? *You* are always on His mind. He considers every detail of your life. He knows your thoughts and feelings, including the ones that even you don't understand. He understands you like no other person can. He knows your strengths and weaknesses, your darkest fears and highest hopes. He's intimately aware of your feelings and interactions throughout each day.

This might be hard truth to wrap your head around: God, the Creator of the universe, doesn't only love you; *He also thinks about you constantly.* He is always with you, waiting for you to turn to Him, to call on Him for help, for friendship, for anything you need.

. . . .

Thank You, Father God, for holding me always in Your thoughts and never forgetting me.

BRAND-NEW

*Therefore, if anyone is in Christ, the new creation
has come: The old has gone, the new is here!*

2 CORINTHIANS 5:17 NIV

Are you in Christ?

That might be a hard question to answer. What exactly does it mean to be "in" Christ? Basically, it means you are in a relationship with Jesus Christ. You talk to Him and share your life with Him. You allow Him to shape your choices; you do your best to practice the love that He showed to everyone. You stop holding so tightly to your life and instead give it freely to Him.

When you're in Christ, you don't have to worry about mistakes you may have made in the past. That's all behind you now! Because you've chosen to have a relationship with Jesus, not only are you *in Him*, but He is also *in you*. You see yourself in a new way now, for the old, selfish you is not the *real* you. In Jesus (through Jesus, with Jesus), you have a brand-new life.

• •

*Jesus, even if I don't quite understand what
it means to be "in You," I do know I want to
follow You. I want to be friends with You.
Thank You for making everything new for me.*

WHEN YOU DON'T FEEL WELL

*Keep a firm grip on the faith. The suffering won't last
forever. It won't be long before this generous God who
has great plans for us in Christ—eternal and glorious
plans they are!—will have you put together and on your
feet for good. He gets the last word; yes, he does.*

1 PETER 5:10–11 MSG

When you don't feel well, it's not only your body that
suffers; your heart (your emotions) and your spirit (the
part of you that interacts with God) suffer too. Physical
pain can wear you down. It can rob you of the pleasure
you normally take in each day. Difficult emotions don't
have to get in the way of your relationship with God,
though. Jesus understands. The Bible makes clear that
Jesus suffered as much emotionally the night before
His death, when He was scared and lonely, as He did
physically when He was actually hanging from the
cross. So if you're not feeling well, don't worry that
God will be upset with you for being sad or scared or
grouchy. You don't need to fight your feelings. Instead,
give them to God. Tell Him all about your feelings, the
ones in your heart as well as in your body. Jesus will
see you through times of sickness or pain—and He will
bring you out on the other side, into the beautiful life
He has planned for you.

*When I don't feel well, Lord Jesus,
remind me that You are with me.*

DON'T LET FEAR GET IN THE WAY

While Jesus was still speaking, some people came from the house of Jairus, the synagogue leader. "Your daughter is dead," they said. "Why bother the teacher anymore?" Overhearing what they said, Jesus told him, "Don't be afraid; just believe."

MARK 5:35–36 NIV

The people of Jesus' day thought death was a dead end. They thought it put a final stop to anything Jesus could do. But Jesus showed them otherwise. He healed Jairus' little girl, proving that with God, there are no dead ends. Jesus wanted to show the people that nothing is impossible for God, and He wants you to learn the same lesson. When the odds seem to be stacked against you, when it looks like things have completely fallen apart, don't be afraid. Give the situation to Jesus, and then wait to see what He will do. He may not do exactly what you imagined or wanted Him to do, but He will always bring new life and hope to every situation, even the ones that seem like dead ends.

* * *

Remind me, Lord, to come to You with every situation and then leave it in Your hands so that You can do something amazing. Don't let my fear get in the way of the things You want to do in my life.

GOD IS IN CONTROL

*"The torrents of destruction overwhelmed me. . . .
In my distress I called to the Lord. . . . From his
temple he heard my voice; my cry came to his ears."*

2 SAMUEL 22:5, 7 NIV

God will never ask you to handle life all by yourself. When your life seems like it's been hit by a hurricane, call out to God for help. He will always hear you. He won't let you be drowned in a sea of trouble or blown away by the winds of life. If you can just hold on a little longer, He will send you help. He has everything under control. Trust Him.

The larger world beyond your personal life can also seem pretty scary. Frightening things seem to happen all the time: murders, environmental damage, diseases, wars, and constant fighting and arguing among people. Again, remember—no matter how messy the world looks, God is always in control. Trust Him.

. . . .

*Teach me, Father God, to give You all my fears
and then leave them with You so that I can have
the joy and peace You want me to have.*

NEW PLACES

The LORD had said to Abram, "Leave your native country, your relatives, and your father's family, and go to the land that I will show you. . . . I will bless you. . .and you will be a blessing to others."
GENESIS 12:1–2 NLT

Sometimes God likes to shake you up a little, stretch you out of your comfort zone, push you out into new experiences. That's not always very comfortable. You may want to stay right where you've been; you may not want to leave old, familiar things and places behind in order to venture out into new and unexplored parts of life.

But as you get older, changes are likely to come at you faster and faster. In not too many years (or months) from now, you may move out of the house where you grew up and go somewhere new, somewhere with different people and different ways of doing things. God promises to bless you there, though. He promises you will grow and discover new things and make new friends. And He has a purpose for you in each change that comes your way. Not only does He want to teach you new things, but He also wants to use you in new ways to bring His love into the world.

. . . .

When it's time for me to travel into a new phase of my life, Father, help me to depend on You. I know that You go with me wherever I go.

PEER PRESSURE

We are not trying to please people
but God, who tests our hearts.

1 Thessalonians 2:4 niv

The teen years are a time when most kids care a lot about the opinions of others. They want other people their age to like them, so they try to act and dress and talk in ways that will help them be accepted. As you get closer to God, though, you'll care less and less about other people's opinions. If the God of the universe has accepted you, why should you care about a bunch of teenagers' peer pressure? When God loves you so much, why would you work so hard to win the approval of other kids your age? God's friendship doesn't depend on the way you dress, the style of your hair, or the makeup you wear. He loves the real you that's deep inside. When you stop caring so much about others' approval, God will help that internal "you"—the part of you where He lives—to match up with the external you, the one other people see.

Father God, You know I can't help but care about other people's opinions of me, but help me to care less and less. I don't want peer pressure to shape my life. Help me to care more about pleasing You than about impressing anyone else.

THE HELPER

"And I will ask the Father, and he will give you another Helper, to be with you forever, even the Spirit of truth. . . . For he dwells with you and will be in you."
JOHN 14:16–17 ESV

Friends and family can offer you support and comfort when life is hard, but ultimately, you will have to face things on your own. No one else can stand in your shoes and experience exactly what you are experiencing. No matter how much you and your family and friends love each other, you can't always totally understand each other's feelings. That realization may leave you feeling lonely and sad. Even Jesus felt that way when His friends didn't understand and left Him to face His fears alone. (You can read this account in Matthew 26:36–46.)

But you are never truly alone. Jesus sent a Helper, one who will always be with you and who will always understand. That Helper is the Holy Spirit. When no one else can take away your loneliness, the Spirit will be there, speaking words of love meant for your ears alone.

. . . .

*Thank You, Jesus, for sending the Holy
Spirit to be with me always.*

BE CAREFUL!

Watch your step. Use your head.
Make the most of every chance you get.
EPHESIANS 5:15–16 MSG

Life is full of dangers and temptations. The Bible never pretends that's not the case. Every day you're alive, you are facing challenges of one sort or another. It's not easy to follow Jesus in a world where life keeps rushing at you, demanding that you do this, buy that, watch this, go there, listen to this, learn that. When things are moving so fast, it's easy to slip into attitudes and behaviors that aren't healthy. So be careful! Take your time, and use the intelligence God gave you to examine things more closely. Life is wonderful and precious—use each moment to celebrate God's love. Don't let your opportunities to grow and to bless others slip away!

. . . .

Remind me, Lord Jesus, to stop and think
before I act or speak. Teach me to be like
You. Use me to spread Your love.

HALF-FULL—OR HALF-EMPTY?

A cheerful disposition is good for your health.
PROVERBS 17:22 MSG

Are you a glass-half-full person or a glass-half-empty person? Scientists have discovered that people who have a positive mindset (seeing the glass as half-full) get sick less often than people who tend to focus on the negative (seeing the glass as half-empty). Cheerful people actually have stronger immune systems. As they get older, they have less heart disease. They even live longer! Thousands of years ago, the author of Proverbs already knew what scientists today are finding through their research.

God doesn't want you to go around with a scowl on your face, and He doesn't want you to see only the gloomy side of life. Instead, He wants to share His joy with you. He wants to hear you laugh and see you smile—and so does the rest of the world.

. . . .

May even the expressions on my face, Father, help others around me to know that You love them. Remind me that sad, mad, bad feelings are contagious, but so are glad, loving, positive ones.

YOUR BODY

Do you not know that your body is a temple of the
Holy Spirit within you, whom you have from God?
1 CORINTHIANS 6:19 ESV

Many young women your age tend to be critical of their bodies. They focus on the negatives—the little bump in the nose, the pimple on the chin, the flat chest, or the frizzy hair. God doesn't want you to focus on what you see as being "wrong" with your body, though. Instead, He wants you to respect and care for your body; He even wants you to love it.

What's more, the Spirit lives inside you, and that makes your body like a temple or a church. God uses your body to reveal Himself to the people around you. And He wants you to be healthy—emotionally, physically, spiritually. He loves your entire being, including your body!

. . . .

Remind me, Holy Spirit, that You live inside me.
When I take care of my body, I'm worshipping You!

THE REAL MEANING OF FAITH

*Now faith is confidence in what we hope for
and assurance about what we do not see.*

HEBREWS 11:1 NIV

Faith in God doesn't mean you can ask Him for a brand-new car and one will magically show up in your driveway. It also doesn't mean you can pray a special person will like you as much as you like him—and expect that person to fall madly in love with you. Faith and wishes are not the same thing.

Instead, faith is trusting God to work everything out in the way that is best for you, best for the people in your life, and best for the kingdom God is building. Faith means putting the future in God's hands. It means giving God control over your life and letting Him do what He wants, knowing that everything He does is done in love.

. . . .

*Teach me more about faith, Lord God.
I want to learn how to trust You more.*

LIVING IN THE NOW

I have learned to be content
whatever the circumstances.

PHILIPPIANS 4:11 NIV

Do you ever find yourself thinking so much about something that's in the future, something you can't wait to happen, that you forget to notice what's in your life *right now*? Or, if you do notice, do you catch yourself complaining and whining because life isn't quite perfect and isn't exactly the way you want it to be? A lot of us have this problem. Instead of thanking God for all the good, fun, beautiful things in our lives, we focus on the little irritations, the problems, the imperfections. We may imagine that once we reach a different stage of our lives, things will be so much better. While it's fine to look forward to the future (after all, God has exciting things in store for you!), God wants you to live in the *now*. He has wonderful things He wants to share with you today.

. . . .

Teach me how to live in each moment, Father God,
and help me not to overlook all the good things, both
big and small, that You are constantly giving to me.

JESUS IS YOUR PEACE

He himself is our peace.
EPHESIANS 2:14 NIV

No matter what's going on in your life, peace is available to you through Jesus. You don't have to be discouraged or frightened. Seek safety in God. Run to Jesus. Don't turn to something else for comfort, like drugs or alcohol or an unhealthy relationship, because while those things might seem to help in the short term, in the long term they cause even more problems. Don't even let seemingly harmless things take Jesus' place in your life—things like your social media accounts, TV, or snacks. Only Jesus can give you the comfort you want and need. He won't instantly make all your problems go away, but He'll change the way you feel about them. His presence inside you will make you stronger, calmer, less worried. He'll help you cope with life.

. . . .

Remind me, Lord Jesus, to find my
comfort and strength only in You.

HANDLE WORRY WITH PRAYER

*Don't fret or worry. Instead of worrying, pray.
Let petitions and praises shape your worries into
prayers, letting God know your concerns. Before
you know it, a sense of God's wholeness, everything
coming together for good, will come and settle
you down. It's wonderful what happens when
Christ displaces worry at the center of your life.*

PHILIPPIANS 4:6–7 MSG

Feeling worried about things is a normal human reaction. Never think that anxiety means you have lost your faith! In fact, God can use your worries to draw you closer to Him, helping you to recognize your needs and limitations as you learn to rely on the only one who always has what you truly need. God doesn't want you to let anxiety destroy the pleasure life gives you, though. Prayer is a practical tool that can help you cope with your worries.

* *

*When I feel worried and upset, Lord Jesus, remind me
to talk to You. Don't let me forget about You or allow
time to slip by without seeking connection with You.*

IN THE MORNING

*In the morning, Lord, you hear my voice; in the morning
I lay my requests before you and wait expectantly.*

PSALM 5:3 NIV

What is the first thing you do each morning? Do you
hit the ground running, already focused on the day
ahead? Or do you pull the covers over your head and
try to catch just a few more minutes of sleep? Either
way, take a minute right now to talk to God about how
He might want you to use your mornings. Prayer isn't
magic, of course, but setting aside a short time each
morning—even a few minutes—to focus on God, giving
the day ahead to Him, can help keep you on track even
on your busiest days. Spending time with God is worth
getting up a few minutes earlier!

. . . .

*Tomorrow morning, Lord, remind me to find a few
minutes to spend with You. Even if it's only when I'm in
the shower or while I'm riding the bus to school, I want
to make sure I connect with You before my day begins.*

BLiND SPOTS

Search me, God, and know my heart; put me to the test and know my anxious thoughts; and see if there is any hurtful way in me, and lead me in the everlasting way.

PSALM 139:23–24 NASB

What is worrying you right now? A relationship? Your busy schedule? Your schoolwork? Or tensions in your family? Whatever it is, you can give it to God. Ask Him to search your heart and discover the root causes of your uneasiness. Since He knows you even better than you know yourself, He can show you if there's any hidden issue you haven't been willing to face. He may want to show you something—an attitude, a habit, a behavior—that is hurtful to you and possibly to others as well as to your relationship with Him. We all have blind spots, areas of ourselves that we can't see. You can't know what you don't know! So ask God to show you.

. . . .

Thank You, Father God, that You can see me clearly, even when I can't, even when I'm totally confused. Show me the way I need to go.

JESUS WAS A TEENAGER!

*For we do not have a high priest who is unable
to empathize with our weaknesses, but we
have one who has been tempted in every
way, just as we are—yet he did not sin.*
HEBREWS 4:15 NIV

A best friend is someone who truly "gets you." She thinks the same things are funny as you do, she listens to you, and she understands and forgives you when you mess up. But even your best friend cannot compare to Jesus. Whatever is bothering you, Jesus always understands. Although you may not have thought of Jesus as an adolescent, He was one! He understands what it's like to have hormones and pimples and wild emotions. He also knows what it's like to be tempted, to want to have power and control, to wish you could just give in and be selfish. (You can read about Jesus being tempted in Luke 4:1–13.) He gets it! And if you feel weak and wobbly, like you're not too certain you can keep following Him, He'll give you the strength to hold on.

· ·

*Thank You, Lord Jesus, that You loved me so
much that You were willing to go through zits
and crazy hormones and everything else that
goes along with being an adolescent.*

NO ONE LEFT OUT

Christ is all, and is in all. Therefore, as God's chosen people, holy and dearly loved, clothe yourselves with compassion, kindness, humility, gentleness and patience.

COLOSSIANS 3:11–12 NIV

No matter how athletic, beautiful, popular, or smart you are, you've probably experienced a time when you were chosen last or even got overlooked entirely. Being left out is one of life's big disappointments. It hurts. The good news is that this feeling isn't part of the world Jesus is building. In the Jesus world—what the Bible calls the kingdom of God or the kingdom of heaven—God's beloved people are kind, gentle, patient, compassionate, and humble. What's more, everyone is chosen. Christ lives in all of us, and no one gets left out. No one.

. . . .

Jesus, thank You that You will never forget me or leave me out. Now please help me to be more like You as I interact with the kids at school. Show me if someone is being left out, and give me the courage to reach out to that person and include her.

WHEN LiFE WEARS YOU DOWN

Have compassion on me, LORD, for I am weak.
PSALM 6:2 NLT

Life can wear you down mentally, physically, spiritually. The adults in your life may not fully realize that even though you're young, you still have responsibilities, problems, and headaches. After dealing with so many things in your busy days, you may be left feeling exhausted. Your thoughts are blurry, your body is limp with tiredness, and you just feel like crying.

Times like those are when you're most vulnerable to temptation. When you're tired, it's easy to snap at someone and hurt their feelings. You also may feel as though you *deserve* to do something that feels good, even though in the long run that thing won't make you happier or healthier. So when you're feeling weak, be extra careful. Tell God how you're feeling and ask Him for His help. He always understands.

. . . .

When I'm tired and worn down, Lord, remind me that I need to depend even more on You.

THE PROMiSED LAND

*LORD, you are my God; I will exalt you and praise
your name, for in perfect faithfulness you have
done wonderful things, things planned long ago.*

ISAIAH 25:1 NIV

God promised the Jewish people that they would have
their own land one day. They clung to that promise,
even when it seemed like it would never come true.
And then, when it did come true, they lost their land
again. It was many centuries before they once again had
their own nation, and the Jewish people went through
many terrible things. It would have been easy to give
up on God, but during those hundreds and hundreds of
years, the Jews always believed that God would keep
His promise to them. And He did.

God has a "promised land" for you too—an awesome plan for your life. Some days, that may seem hard
to believe, but God always keeps His promises. Always.

*Father, You know I sometimes have a hard time
believing that You have a plan for my life. There are
days when everything seems like such a mess. Help me
to keep trusting You the way Your people, the Jews, did.*

STAND STILL!

"The Lord will fight for you; you need only to be still."
EXODUS 14:14 NIV

In this verse, Moses is commanding God's people, the Israelites, to stop panicking and stand still. The Israelites had been slaves in Egypt, but now they had just been released from bondage and were trekking through the wilderness. There was a big problem, though—their former masters were chasing them! When Moses told them to stop moving and stand still, it must have seemed like really bad advice. But God held back the waters of the Red Sea, and the Israelites were able to walk across on dry ground, leaving the Egyptians behind them.

Do you ever stress and panic, racking your brain trying to figure out a solution to a problem? Next time, instead of running around in circles accomplishing very little, try standing still and praying. Moses lived nearly four thousand years ago—but his advice is still good today.

. . . .

The next time I'm upset and nervous, Lord God, remind me to stand still and let You fight my battles.

YOUR LIFE PRESERVER

My comfort in my suffering is this:
Your promise preserves my life.
PSALM 119:50 NIV

In the difficulties of life, God is like a life preserver. When you're battered by the waves of life, tossed up and down until you're certain you're going to drown, God will keep you afloat. God is immune to the troubles that bother you so much, and He can help you float on your problems the way a life preserver floats on the waves. The waves will still toss you around, but with a life preserver, you'll never sink.

God not only understands what you're going through, but He also reaches out to help you. The Bible is full of wonderful promises to you—promises of love and safety and guidance—and God will keep every last one of those promises. You can count on Him. He won't let you drown.

. . . .

Thank You, Father God, that no matter what
I'm going through, You're always there with me.
When life is too hard for me to handle, You keep
me from sinking. You literally save my life.

JUST BREATHE!

"Oh, that I had the wings of a dove!
I would fly away and be at rest."
PSALM 55:6 NIV

No matter how much you know with your head about God's strength and love, and no matter how much you've grown spiritually, sometimes your body betrays you. Your muscles are tense, preparing for a battle that you have no ability to fight. When you try to rest, your head pounds and your stomach hurts. Even though you try to pray, your body just doesn't cooperate. Your hands are sweaty, your breath comes fast, and you can't relax. You can't get rid of that nervous feeling in your gut.

But God is there, even in those moments. Take slow, deep breaths. Imagine yourself inhaling God's love and exhaling all your tension. Don't try to think or pray beyond that. Simply breathe—in, out, in, out, in, out—one breath at a time.

. . . .

I breathe in Your love, Lord.
I breathe out all my anxiety.

GIVE IT ALL TO GOD

*Why, my soul, are you downcast? Why so
disturbed within me? Put your hope in God,
for I will yet praise him, my Savior and my God.*

PSALM 42:11 NIV

Everyone experiences times when frustrations seem
to outweigh joys. As a follower of Jesus, though, you
have an unending source of encouragement in God.
That's great, you may think, *but how do I actually* feel
that joy the Bible talks about so much?

The first step is to pray. Share your stress, frustrations, and worries with God. Don't hold back; even
if you're angry with God, let Him know.

Once you've fully vented your feelings, the next
step is to imagine God taking them in His hands. "Let
Me hold these for you now," He says, "just for a little
while. If you want them back later, you can have them,
but for now, let Me carry them for you."

Finally, the third step is to take some time to
think about all that is good in your life. Make a list on
paper if you need to. Spend time focusing on all these
good things. Thank God for them. Ask Him to help you
find more room in your life for the things that make
you happy.

. . . .

*When I'm overwhelmed with my life, Lord God, remind
me that what I need most is to spend time with You.*

LOOK AT THE FLOWERS

"Consider how the wild flowers grow. They do not labor or spin. Yet I tell you, not even Solomon in all his splendor was dressed like one of these. If that is how God clothes the grass of the field, which is here today, and tomorrow is thrown into the fire, how much more will he clothe you—you of little faith!"

LUKE 12:27–28 NIV

If God makes the flowers, each type unique and beautiful, and if He sends the rain and sun to meet their needs, will He not care for you as well? That's what Jesus is saying in these verses. God made you—and what the Creator made, He loves. . .and that which He loves, He cares for. You are made in God's image. You are dear to Him. Rest in Him. Trust Him. Just as He cares for the birds and the flowers—as well as the bugs and the furry four-legged creatures and the fish and even microscopic creatures too tiny for us to see—God will take care of you.

. . . .

Creator, thank You for making me, thank You for loving me, thank You for caring for me. Help me to trust You more.

DON'T BE DISCOURAGED!

Therefore we do not lose heart. . . .
We are being renewed day by day.
2 CORINTHIANS 4:16 NIV

Sometimes it's hard to hang on. You might have thought you knew what to expect when you accepted a responsibility, but the reality has turned out to be heavier and more complicated than you imagined. Or you've gotten yourself involved with a group of people who, you discover now, want to pressure you into doing things you're not comfortable doing. Don't be discouraged. God is still with you. He will build your faith, your energy, and your courage even in situations like these. No matter what you've gotten yourself into, He'll still be there with you.

During challenging times, holding on is really all you have to do. This period in your life won't last forever. Tell yourself you can hold on one more minute, one more hour, one more day—and you will. Lean on God, and He'll show the way through your situation.

I'm so glad, Father God, that You never judge me. Even when I make mistakes, You stay with me. Show me how to keep on following You even when I get myself in situations that are hard for me to handle.

BE THE BEST YOU CAN BE

*Then, because so many people were coming
and going that they did not even have a chance
to eat, he said to them, "Come with me by
yourselves to a quiet place and get some rest."*

MARK 6:31 NIV

Do you ever have days when you're so busy you never
even stop to eat? Jesus had days like that too when He
was on earth. You might think Jesus would have just
kept on going. After all, couldn't He have just called
on His Father for some extra energy and strength? But
Jesus didn't do that. Instead, He accepted the needs
and limitations of His human body. He knew that we
serve God best when we take care of our bodies—when
we get enough sleep, when we eat healthy regular
meals, and when we take time to relax. He made sure
He and His friends prioritized rest.

As tempting as it may be sometimes to skip meals
or cut your sleeping hours, if you do, you won't be at
your best—and God loves for you to be at your best!

*Help me not to be so busy, Lord, that I don't
have time to do the things that will keep me healthy.
As a young adult, I know that taking care of myself
is my job now. I want to be the best I can be.*

CONNECTED TO THE VINE

*"I am the true vine, and My Father is the vinedresser.
. . . Remain in Me, and I in you. Just as the branch
cannot bear fruit of itself but must remain in the
vine, so neither can you unless you remain in Me."*

JOHN 15:1, 4 NASB

Jesus liked to use word pictures to explain Himself. In these verses, He compares Himself to a vine—and He says that you are like a branch of that vine. If a branch is cut off from the vine, it will soon turn brown and die. It can't live on its own. But when the branch stays connected to the vine, it grows strong and healthy. The vine draws up water and nutrients from the soil and passes them along to each one of its branches, so that together they just keep growing and growing and growing.

*Jesus, I want to be like the branch connected to the
vine—I want to be connected to You. I want to absorb
the life You give so that I can grow and so that my life
bears the "fruit" that will help others to know You too.*

FLY!

But those who trust in the LORD will find new strength.
They will soar high on wings like eagles. They will run
and not grow weary. They will walk and not faint.
ISAIAH 40:31 NLT

When we experience any kind of weakness—whether emotional, spiritual, intellectual, or physical—it can be hard to take. We would all rather impress people with our strength, talents, and skills than expose the ways we're not strong, not talented, not skilled. We don't like to admit when we can't do something. Most of us would really like to be *better* than our friends.

But when you accept that there are things you can't do, and you rely on God instead, He will give you new strength. He might do this by helping you see the situation differently. He might bring someone into your life who can help you in the areas where you're weak. He might simply use your weakness as a chance to draw you even closer to Him. In the end, you may never be as strong in certain areas of your life as you are in others—but even so, God will help you to *fly*!

Help me, Father God, to let go of my need to be strong, to be better and faster and smarter than other people. Teach me to accept who I am even as I turn to You for new strength. I want to fly with You!

TAKE HEART

"In this world you will have trouble. But take heart! I have overcome the world."

JOHN 16:33 NIV

"Take heart" means to find courage. (The word *courage* also has the French word for heart inside it.) The word *take*, however, implies that this is something you have to participate in. You can't just sit there doing nothing, waiting for Jesus to dump some courage inside you. You have to do something; you have to take action. Jesus overcame the world, and now you have to do your part: you have to take what He is offering you—a new way of living in Him. When you accept this life, the world's troubles won't weigh you down so much because you'll see them from a new point of view. You will start looking at things through the lens of God's love.

. . . .

Jesus, thank You that Your life shows me how to live.

GOD'S PROMISES

For no matter how many promises God has made,
they are "Yes" in Christ. And so through him the
"Amen" is spoken by us to the glory of God.

2 CORINTHIANS 1:20 NIV

A promise says something about the future. It's a commitment to do something, a statement of a fact that has not yet come to pass. The Bible is full of God's promises, His statements of all that He will do for you. Even the beauties and wonders of the natural world—like rainbows—can remind you that God has promised to be faithful to you, to give you life instead of death, to shower you with good things, and to love you for eternity. Nothing can shake the promises of God. He loves to say "Yes!" to life, "Yes!" to hope, and "Yes!" to *you!*

. . . .

Thank You, Father God, for all Your promises
in the Bible. I'm so glad that each one of those
promises is a "yes," not a "no," because You always
lead me into a fuller, healthier, happier life.

HAVE FUN!

A happy heart makes the face cheerful.
PROVERBS 15:13 NIV

Jesus never said He wanted His followers to walk around acting serious and sober all the time. He knew that His love was going to cost Him His life, yet He still told jokes and enjoyed good times with His friends. And now He offers you a life of joy, a joy that will live inside you even when you're going through tough times. So go ahead—have fun! Jesus loves to hear you giggle with your friends; He's delighted when He sees you having a good time. Just remember to include Him, and He will help you make sure that your fun is always loving and never hurtful to you or anyone else.

. . . .

Guide me, Jesus, into the kind of fun that opens me up to You and others, the kind of fun that leads to deeper relationships. And help me to avoid getting caught up in anything that could lead to danger or harm.

GOD'S CREATIVITY

*"My grace is all you need. My power
works best in weakness."*

2 Corinthians 12:9 nlt

When you feel as though you don't have what it takes to do something, you may feel frustrated or embarrassed. You may be so critical of yourself that your self-concept drops into the mud. You measure yourself against what others can do, and you think you come up lacking.

But that's not how God sees things. If you stop focusing on your own failures and flaws and instead turn your eyes to God, He'll have a chance to demonstrate His power. His love and strength will flow into your life. As you rely on Him, instead of worrying so much about yourself, you will grow closer to Him. The same God who made the universe is as powerful and creative as ever—and when you stop trying to do things by yourself, He will have room to create something wonderful in your life.

*Creator, I want to give You my life, my whole
self, including all the things I don't like very
much about myself. Please use all the pieces
of my life to create something beautiful.*

CONNECTED TO GOD

Rejoice always, pray continually,
give thanks in all circumstances.

1 THESSALONIANS 5:16–18 NIV

How could God possibly expect you to *always* rejoice, pray, and give Him thanks? Does He want you to walk around with a smile on your face even when terrible things are happening in the world? Are you supposed to go through your day with your eyes closed and your lips moving as you talk to God? How do you make sense of verses like these?

Let's start by looking at the word *rejoice*. We usually think of rejoicing as having to do with celebration and joy. But the Bible meaning of the word has more to do with being whole and healthy, living your life in connection with God, who is the source of all life. You do this by following the direction in the next two verses: First, pray continually, which means you keep the lines of communication always open between you and God. Second, another way to be in connection with God is to notice all the little and big things He's done for you—and to thank Him! These are the ways you "rejoice always."

. . . .

Please keep teaching me, Lord, how to
make our connection even stronger.

RESCUE

*Then I will rejoice in the LORD. I will be
glad because he rescues me.*

PSALM 35:9 NLT

Do you ever feel as though you're waiting for someone
to come and rescue you from your life? You might
think a parent will rescue you, or a boyfriend, or a
special teacher. You wait and wait and wait. . . But
God doesn't want you to exist in a perpetual state
of waiting for someone to come along and help you.
He wants to rescue you *now.* When you follow Jesus,
He will show *you* how to overcome the problems in
your life. You may need to ask for help from friends,
family, or teachers, but asking for help can actually
be a way you and God begin to take charge of your
life. You don't have to sit around waiting any longer.

*Father God, You make me happy. I'm so grateful You
are with me right now. Right this second, You are
already rescuing me from all the messes in my life.*

HURT FEELiNGS

Bear with each other and forgive one another.
COLOSSIANS 3:13 NIV

People often feel awkward in the presence of others' pain. They don't know what to say. Sometimes they say silly things that seem hurtful. Or they may be so worried they'll say the wrong thing that they say nothing at all, and that can hurt too. You've probably been on both sides of this situation: you've been the one longing for your friends' understanding and sympathy; and you've been the one who didn't know how to give comfort and encouragement when a friend was going through a hard time. Even close friends sometimes let each other down, and when that happens, both people hurt.

That's why the Bible tells us to be patient and forgiving with each other. We're all still learning, still growing. We need to forgive each other for not being perfect—especially since God always forgives us.

When I'm having trouble forgiving a friend who hurt me, Lord, remind me that I'm not perfect either.

YOUR THOUGHTS

*We take captive every thought to
make it obedient to Christ.*

2 CORINTHIANS 10:5 NIV

Your thoughts shape your life. If you think you can't do something, it's unlikely that you'll even try it. Negative thoughts can hold you back. Even worse, your thoughts tell lies sometimes. They say things like *I'm so ugly. I'm so stupid. What an idiot I am.* Your thoughts remind you of times when you failed, and they insist that you're going to fail again.

Psychologists have learned that thoughts are powerful. But they've also learned that people can *choose* what they think. By paying attention to what your mind is saying to you, you can learn to talk back to its criticisms. You can call out the lies and replace them with the truth of God's love for you. That's what 2 Corinthians 10:5 means when it says to "take captive every thought." Make your thoughts quiet; don't let them boss you around anymore, and obey Jesus' command to love others as you also love yourself (Mark 12:31).

* *

*Jesus, please teach me how to control my
thoughts so that they become obedient to
You, speaking Your truth, Your love.*

ONE STEP AT A TIME

Show me the way I should go,
for to you I entrust my life.
PSALM 143:8 NIV

Wouldn't it be nice if God would make it absolutely clear which direction you should go in life? Maybe He could write a message across the sky or send you some other miraculous sign. But that's seldom the way God works. Instead, God usually shows us the way just one step at a time. Then as you follow Him, giving Him everything, you'll notice you begin to have a new perspective on life. Things you once thought you absolutely *had* to have won't seem as important, while other things you might have once overlooked or laughed at become necessary. You may see new opportunities you never considered before.

But none of this will happen if you cling tight to your own old way of doing things. You have to let go, and then God will show you the next step to take.

. . . .

I want to give You my life, Lord, but I know sometimes
I grab it back again. No matter how many times
I do that, help me each time to get back on track
quickly, following You one step at a time.

LET IT GO

"Martha, Martha," the Lord answered, "you are worried and upset about many things, but few things are needed—or indeed only one."
LUKE 10:41–42 NIV

Martha was busy. When Jesus and His friends came to dinner, she ran around frantically, getting the food ready, making sure her guests were happy. Maybe she hoped to impress Jesus with her home and her cooking. Meanwhile, though, her sister, Mary, just sat at Jesus' feet, listening to Him talk and doing absolutely nothing to help Martha. No wonder Martha was upset! But Jesus reminded her that she needed to let go of all the things that were worrying her. Relationships are far more important to the kingdom of God than perfectly prepared meals or a beautiful house (or pretty much anything else). And here's the message for *you*: You don't need to try to impress people. Instead, you can practice loving them the way Jesus does.

. . . .

Jesus, You are more important to me than anything else. Help me to let go of my need to impress others so that I can listen to You. I want to be more like You.

THE WORLD'S VOICE

*If all you want is your own way, flirting
with the world every chance you get,
you end up enemies of God and his way.*

JAMES 4:4 MSG

When the Bible talks about the "world," it means a way of thinking and living that is not based on God's love. The world you live in today says money, power, and fame are more important than love. It says that working to get ahead is more important than helping someone else. Even though you've decided to follow Jesus, it's still easy to soak up these attitudes and values. That's why this verse warns you not to flirt with the world. The world has a loud voice that's shouting its selfish messages everywhere—online, on TV, in commercials, in the magazines you read, and even in conversations with friends. The world's voice is far louder than the voice of the Holy Spirit, which is always soft and gentle. The world's voice can nudge you off the path God wants you to follow. But you don't have to listen!

*Holy Spirit, today I don't want to listen to
the world's voice—I want to hear Yours.*

FOCUS ON JESUS

Keep your eyes on Jesus, who both began
and finished this race we're in.
HEBREWS 12:2 MSG

When you feel confused and overwhelmed, there is only one thing you need to do: focus on Jesus. Think about Him. Talk to Him. Read about Him in your Bible. The more you "keep your eyes" on Him, the calmer you'll feel. When you focus on Him, you take strength from Him.

Remember, you're not doing this thing called life on your own. Jesus was there at the very beginning when you took your first breath, when you were just a baby. Jesus was also there at the beginning of your spiritual life, when you first decided to follow Him. And Jesus isn't going to leave you now. As you keep your eyes on Him, He will go with you every step of the way, through every trouble, until the day you finally see Him face-to-face.

. . . .

Jesus, today I want to keep my focus on You
no matter what is going on around me. When
my attention wanders, pull me back to You.

ANGRY WORDS

I urge Euodia and I urge Syntyche to live in harmony in the Lord.

PHILIPPIANS 4:2 NASB

Euodia and Syntyche were two women in the church at Philippi and apparently they were quarreling. Maybe Euodia said something that hurt Syntyche's feelings. When Syntyche let Euodia know how upset she was, Euodia got defensive. And after that, the situation just got worse and worse.

When the apostle Paul wrote a letter to the Philippian church (this letter later became the book of Philippians in the Bible), he took time to mention this tiff between two women. He had a lot of other important things to say, but Paul knew relationships are important to the kingdom of God. When we don't get along with each other, we hurt God's kingdom.

God cares about your relationships too. He thinks angry words between friends should be addressed and resolved. He asks that you do everything you can to get along with everyone so that your life shows others Jesus' love.

. . . .

Forgive me, Jesus, for the times I'm mean or resentful. Remind me that my job is to help build Your kingdom here on earth so that more and more people can come together and share Your love.

BE FAIR!

"Be just and fair to all. Do what is right and good, for I am coming soon to rescue you and to display my righteousness among you."

ISAIAH 56:1 NLT

Fairness is important to God. He wants you to work with Him to build a world that's fair for everyone—a world where everyone is loved and welcomed no matter what they look like or what they believe. You can help with this by speaking up when you notice something that's unfair, rather than assuming that someone else—a teacher or another adult—will take care of the problem. You defend anyone who is being bullied or insulted. When people tell hurtful jokes, you don't laugh. When you hear people referring to other groups of people with insulting names, you don't join in. You work hard to be like Jesus—fair and kind to everyone.

. . . .

Jesus, I want to work with You to build a world where everyone is safe, welcomed, and valued.

GiFTS FROM JESUS

God is strong, and he wants you strong. So take everything the Master has set out for you, well-made weapons of the best materials. And put them to use.

EPHESIANS 6:10–11 MSG

In this verse, the Bible is using a metaphor to help you understand a deeper meaning. It's comparing your relationship with Jesus to the relationship of a soldier with his leader. Soldiers don't have to buy or make their own weapons; instead, weapons are given to them, and they are expected to put those weapons to use. Here's the takeaway: you don't have to make yourself spiritually strong, nor do you have to make yourself "good." But if your hands are already full of your own "stuff," you won't be able to take the "weapons" (against selfishness and cruelty and hatred) Jesus wants to give you. You need to set all your things down—let them go—so you can accept the gifts of life Jesus is offering you.

. . . .

Jesus, thank You for giving me everything I need to face life. Remind me to take Your gifts—and use them.

CLOUDS

"Listen to this, Job; stop and consider God's wonders. Do you know how God controls the clouds and makes his lightning flash? Do you know how the clouds hang poised, those wonders of him who has perfect knowledge?"

JOB 37:14–16 NIV

"Stop and think about the wonderful things I've done," God told Job. Then He pointed to something that must have seemed pretty ordinary to Job at first glance: the clouds. But if you've ever lain on your back watching the clouds—or looked at them from an airplane's window—you know that clouds can be amazing and wonderful. They're like a work of art in the sky, one that's constantly changing its shapes and colors.

Job had gone through some major hard times, and God's advice, basically, was "Spend some time just looking at the world of nature, Job." Maybe you should try it too. The next time life seems like too much for you to handle, spend some time just looking at the clouds. See if there's anything God wants to say to you through that amazing art show in the sky.

Thank You, Lord, for making such a beautiful world. Remind me not to take it for granted.

NATURE SPEAKS

The heavens proclaim the glory of God. The skies display his craftsmanship. Day after day they continue to speak; night after night they make him known.

PSALM 19:1–2 NLT

Here again, the Bible is reminding you that God can speak to you through the world of nature. He has woven His creative love throughout nature. Sunsets, seashells, flowers, snowflakes, shining water, moonlit nights, starry skies, birdsong, trees—all of these beautiful things are right in front of you, gifts of beauty God has given you.

Even if it's in your own backyard or a park, spend some time in nature. Find a quiet place to clear your head and draw close to God. Outdoor places are good for prayer, and God may have something He wants to whisper to you through the murmur of the wind in the trees, the warmth of the sun on your face, and even the scent of soil and growing things. If you listen, nature always speaks about God.

. . . .

Thank You, Creator, for the beautiful world You made. Remind me to pay attention to skies and trees, animals and birds. Let's spend some time together outdoors soon!

FAILURES AND FALLS

*To him who is able to keep you from stumbling
and to present you before his glorious
presence without fault and with great joy.*

JUDE 24 NIV

Jesus loves you unconditionally. You don't have to earn
His love by being good. You don't have to prove that
you're strong or talented or beautiful. All you have to
do is depend on Jesus. He is the one who can keep you
from falling—from making mistakes that send you off
the path God wants you to follow. And if you do fall,
no matter how big the fall might be, no matter how
ashamed and embarrassed and guilty you feel, you can
come to Jesus to be lifted up and healed.

So don't worry about trying to impress either God
or others. You are already loved and accepted just as
you are. Just keep following Jesus, and He will never
stop showing you the right way to go.

* *

*Jesus, when I trip up and hurt someone or myself,
thank You that You still love me and will lead me back
onto Your path and help me to do better next time.*

MONEY

Command those who are rich. . .not to be arrogant nor to put their hope in wealth, which is so uncertain, but to put their hope in God, who richly provides us with everything for our enjoyment.

1 TIMOTHY 6:17 NIV

God gives us so many things to enjoy, including things that cost money, like houses and cars, nice clothes and computer games. It's not wrong to enjoy these things, but if you make them more important to you than God is, they will never make you truly happy. Having a lot of things doesn't make you a better person—and having fewer things doesn't mean you're not as good as everyone else.

Everything in your life comes from God. You can't claim any of it as proof of your value. God loves to give you good gifts, but He never wants you to love the gift more than the Giver. He is the source of all your happiness.

. . . .

Thank You, Father God, for all the wonderful things in my life. Teach me to enjoy them without making them more important to me than You are.

WITH GOD'S HELP

With your help I can advance against a troop; with my God I can scale a wall.

PSALM 18:29 NIV

Do you ever become discouraged when you face an enormous task? Whether it's learning to play a musical instrument, writing a paper for history class, or cleaning your room for the first time in many months, the size of the job can fool you into thinking it's impossible. But God can help you do what you didn't think could be done.

So say a prayer and then get to work. Tasks like these are best faced one step at a time; instead of trying to move an entire mountain of work, chip away at it little by little. When you're patient and don't give up, with God's help, you may be surprised by how quickly you finish.

. . . .

I am so grateful, Lord, for Your help and strength. Help me to be patient and willing to take baby steps in order to achieve my goals.

HOLDING GOD'S HAND

*When he falls, he will not be hurled down, because
the Lord is the One who holds his hand.*

PSALM 37:24 NASB

One day you're filled with energy, ready to go out and change the world—and the next day you're so discouraged and sad you can barely move. Life is like that, especially when you're an adolescent. Teenage hormones can exaggerate your emotions, turning good things into amazing, exhilarating pleasure. . .and bad things into the end of the world. When you compare your sadness and discouragement today to the excitement you felt yesterday, you may feel guilty, as though you've done something wrong. You haven't! God is just as close to you when you're sad and frustrated and worried as He is when you're overflowing with happiness and energy. It *feels* better to be happy, but whether you're happy or sad, God loves you just the same. He may even have things He wants to teach you through the difficult days. He'll never stop holding your hand.

. . . .

*God of love, I'm so glad You are always
with me, always holding my hand.*

A FULL CUP

*"I am coming to you now, but I say these things
while I am still in the world, so that they may
have the full measure of my joy within them."*

JOHN 17:13 NIV

Imagine you have an empty cup in your hands. You
hold your cup up to Jesus so He can fill it up with some
delicious beverage. Jesus begins to pour the drink into
your cup, but when your cup is half full, you say, "That's
enough, Jesus. I don't want any more."

Jesus is disappointed. "But I wanted to fill it to
the top," He says to you. "I wanted to fill it until it
overflowed."

Jesus has so many things He wants to give you.
He has already given you a lot, but there is even more
He's yearning to make yours. Will you let Him fill your
"cup" until it runs over?

. . . .

*Jesus, I'm sorry if I've been rejecting gifts You long
to give me. Show me if there's something in me
that's holding me back from accepting everything
that's mine through You. Maybe something in me
is scared. Let's figure this out together, Lord.*

WHAT'S YOUR SPIRITUAL LOCATION?

Those who live in the shelter of the Most High will find rest in the shadow of the Almighty. This I declare about the LORD: He alone is my refuge, my place of safety; he is my God, and I trust him.

PSALM 91:1–2 NLT

If something is getting you down, check your spiritual location. Are you close to God, sheltered by His love? Or have you wandered off, forgetting about God, and now you realize you feel very far away from Him?

In reality, God hasn't gone anywhere. He never leaves your side. But even though He's right there with you, as close as ever, you can't see Him because you've given all your attention to something or someone else. You haven't been spending time with God, you haven't been thinking about Him, and now it's no wonder life looks gloomy.

So turn around. God is right there, waiting for you to return to Him.

* *

Thank You, Father God, that You never leave my side. Forgive me for the times I forget You and turn away from You. I'm so grateful Your love is always there, ready to shelter me.

THE KINGDOM OF GOD

"Your kingdom come."
MATTHEW 6:10 NIV

Jesus described His Father's kingdom in many ways. It's like scattered seed, He said (Matthew 13:1–9); in other words, it starts out as a tiny something that's sprinkled everywhere in our world, ready to grow. The kingdom is also like a wheat field, Jesus said, that one day will nourish us with food (13:24–30); it's a mustard seed (13:31–32), which has the potential to grow into something tall; it's like yeast in bread dough, making our world bubble and expand (13:33). The kingdom is a treasure, a pearl that's precious and valuable (13:44–46); it's a net (13:47–50) that sweeps up and includes everything and everyone; and finally, it's a wedding feast (22:2), a wonderful party.

When you pray these words from the Lord's Prayer—"Your kingdom come"—*that's* what you're asking for.

. . . .

Jesus, I didn't understand exactly what You meant when You talked about Your Father's "kingdom," but the little I can understand sounds amazing. I want to work with You to make Your kingdom visible to everyone.

WORKING FOR GOD

Whatever you do, work at it with all your heart,
as working for the Lord, not for human masters.
COLOSSIANS 3:23 NIV

You probably enjoy some of the work you do but don't like other work quite as much. You might be very interested in some of your classes, which makes your homework more interesting as well. Meanwhile, you're *not* interested in other classes, and you get bored doing the homework. You might hate having to do chores at home when you'd much rather be out having fun with your friends. But God wants you to give your whole self to whatever work you do. Find ways to connect with even your boring tasks. When you're doing cleaning chores, imagine that Jesus is coming to your house as a guest. When you do your homework, picture Jesus checking your work. Do all your work for Him!

. . . .

Father God, when I'm stuck in the middle
of what seems like a boring job, remind me
that all my work is really done for You.

REMEMBERING

*"Remember that you were slaves in Egypt and that the L*ORD *your God brought you out of there with a mighty hand and an outstretched arm."*

DEUTERONOMY 5:15 NIV

When God's people looked back at all the wonderful ways He had helped them in the past, they were encouraged to face both the present and the future. If you feel discouraged with your life today, you too can take some time to remember all the things God has done for you, ever since you were a child. When you look back, you'll see all the ways God was there with you, even in your worst times, and how He used even those bad times to help you learn and grow. Right now, as you turn to God for help, you are building strength that will help you down the road. Each time God helps you, it's like a link in a chain that just keeps growing longer and stronger.

Lord God, please remind me of all the things You did for me while I was growing up, and thank You for all the things You're doing in my life right now.

TRUST FALL

"The Lord himself goes before you and will be with you; he will never leave you nor forsake you. Do not be afraid; do not be discouraged."

DEUTERONOMY 31:8 NIV

Have you ever done that exercise in trust where you fall backward into another person's arms? It's hard to let yourself drop, trusting that the other person will catch you. No matter how well you know the other person, something inside you keeps saying, *But what if they let me fall?* If you do the exercise a few times in a row, though, each time it's a little easier to believe that the other person will catch you.

It can be hard to let your life fall into God's hands too, trusting that He will hold it safe. If you're like most people, you want to be in control of things. It feels scary to give control of your life to God instead. But each time you do, it gets a little easier. You start to realize that your life is safest when it's in God's hands.

* *

Sometimes it's hard to trust You, Lord, but I'm trying. Teach me to trust You more and more.

THE SAME POWER

The Spirit of God, who raised Jesus
from the dead, lives in you.
ROMANS 8:11 NLT

God is the same yesterday, today, and forever. That means He can still do amazing things now just like He did in the past. When you read stories in the Bible about all the ways God helped and healed people, you can claim those stories for yourself. You can learn from them and be encouraged by them. The very same power that created the world, led Moses and the Israelites out of slavery, inspired David to write poetry, gave Solomon (the author of Proverbs) astounding wisdom, and raised Jesus from the dead still exists today—and even better, it *lives inside you.*

. . . .

I can hardly believe, Father, that Your amazing
power lives inside me. Please, Holy Spirit, shine
Your love through me, out into the world.

SOMETHING BETTER

In their hearts humans plan their course,
but the LORD establishes their steps.

PROVERBS 16:9 NIV

Do you ever get up on a Saturday morning, excited about the day ahead—only to have your plans upset by other people? Maybe it turns out your mom has to take your little brother to a friend's house, so she's not available to drive you where you'd hoped to go. A friend you were counting on as part of your plan texts to say she can't make it after all. And then, while you're trying to find a way to make your plan still work out somehow, your grandparents show up. As much as you love them, you hadn't planned on spending your Saturday entertaining two senior citizens.

But it's likely your day turned out exactly the way God wanted. If you can be flexible enough to let go of your own plans, you may discover God has something even better in mind.

• •

When things don't work out the way I want,
Lord, remind me that You are in control of all
the details of my life, and You always know what
You're doing. I want to respond to others with
love, even when my plans get interrupted.

THE WORD OF GOD

Your word is a lamp for my feet, a light on my path.
PSALM 119:105 NIV

God's Word is the expression of who He is. The Bible is God's Word, and so is Jesus. By reading the Bible and by paying especially close attention to all the things Jesus did and said in the Gospels (Matthew, Mark, Luke, and John), you not only can get to know God better but also can gain insight into how you should live your life. God's Word is like a flashlight, shining into your life so that you see things more clearly. As you make decisions for your future—committing to a sport or a musical instrument, picking a college or a job, or choosing someone to have a serious relationship with—the light of God's Word can help you make the right choices.

*When I feel confused about my life, Father,
remind me to look for answers in Your Word.*

CRYING OUT TO GOD

I call to God, I cry to God to help me. From his palace he hears my call; my cry brings me right into his presence—a private audience!
PSALM 18:6 MSG

You might not ask for God's help until you're truly desperate—but you don't have to wait! In the Bible, whenever we read that someone cries out to God, it is also an expression of their faith and trust. Just as a baby cries, knowing the sound of her voice will bring her mother to her, crying out to God says that you're confident He loves you and know He has the strength to help you.

And God always hears your cries. The Bible is filled with stories about God answering the cries of His people. Like a loving mother, He comes to you when you cry out to Him. He will not leave you to cry alone.

Thank You, Lord God, that You always hear me, and You always help.

LEAVE ROOM FOR FUN

A twinkle in the eye means joy in the heart,
and good news makes you feel fit as a fiddle.
PROVERBS 15:30 MSG

As you get older, you may find your schedule gets busier and busier. What with school and homework, after-school activities like sports and clubs, a part-time job, and volunteer activities at your church or in your community, you may look around and realize that your once-fun life is now not so much fun because it's just *too busy*. God doesn't want you to be worn out and stressed out, though. A little relaxation, recreation, and fun are essential to a healthy life.

So make some time for fun this week! All the other things in your life can wait. When you return to them, you'll find you bring with you more energy than you had before.

· ·

Thank You, Father, for all the activities I'm involved
in. May I learn from each one and use each one as
an opportunity to make this world a better place.
But remind me also that I need to leave room in my
schedule for just having fun with my friends and family.

WAITING FOR GOD

I will wait for the LORD. . . . I will put my trust in him.
ISAIAH 8:17 NIV

Do you wish you could have instant, automatic joy without any heartache? Or do you long for peace without having to cope with life's stress? Do you want to be a good person, a strong and loving person, without ever having to encounter any challenges? Unfortunately, life doesn't work that way. Instead, you'll have opportunities to learn and grow through all life's delays, irritations, struggles, and disappointments. Like the prophet Isaiah, who wrote this verse, you'll need to learn the skill of waiting for God's timing. He will come through for you every time but in *His* time, not yours. Your wait could be hours or days; it might even be years. But God always comes through. All you have to do is wait.

* *

You know I get impatient, Lord. I wish life wasn't so hard sometimes. Help me to be patient. Teach me to trust You, knowing that Your timing is always right.

you MATTER!

*When I look at the night sky and see the work of your
fingers—the moon and the stars you set in place—
what are mere mortals that you should think about
them, human beings that you should care for them?*
PSALM 8:3–4 NLT

The next time you're looking up at a starry sky, think
about this for a moment: *You are God's daughter.*
You are important to the one who made the sun, the
moon, and the stars. The vastness of space is too great
to comprehend. We don't even know how many galaxies are out there; the Hubble telescope has identified
100 billion of them, but scientists believe that the
total number of galaxies is probably more like 2 *tril-
lion.* Now think of all the stars within those trillions
of galaxies, all the planets, all the possible worlds. By
comparison, your life is tiny.

And yet it's infinitely precious to God. Even set
against the hugeness of the universe, you *matter.*

. . . .

*Thank You, God, that in the great expanse
of space, You never lose sight of me.*

THE ONE AND ONLY YOU

*You made all the delicate, inner parts of my body
and knit me together in my mother's womb.*
PSALM 139:13 NLT

At the moment of your conception, your parents' DNA came together, and roughly three million decisions were made about you. Everything from your eye color to the texture of your hair, to your ability to use your right or left hand, to whether you like or hate cilantro—all of it was determined in the blink of an eye.

God was present at that moment, just as He was present at the creation of the universe. And just as the angels sang with joy when the stars were made, they also sang when you came into being. Your life comes from a God who is absolutely head-over-heels crazy in love with you. No one else can love Him or serve Him in quite the same way you can.

. . . .

*Thank You, Lord God, for making me, for
loving me, for having a purpose for me.*

FREE FROM SHAME

*Because the Sovereign L*ORD* helps me, I will not be disgraced. . . . I know that I will not be put to shame.*

ISAIAH 50:7 NLT

Shame is a terrible, secret feeling that something is wrong with you. It can attach itself to you because of old wounds you've been carrying since childhood—or it might come from something that has happened more recently. Either way, shame convinces you that you're worthless, that you're *bad.*

When Jesus was killed on a cross, it was considered a shameful way to die. Only the worst criminals were executed that way. The Bible says, though, that Jesus "endured the cross, scorning its shame" (Hebrews 12:2 NIV). Jesus fully experienced the pain of dying, but He refused to carry the shame. He was being treated as a person with no value, but He knew that shame is always a lie.

No matter what happened to you or what you've done, you are not worthless or bad. How could you be, when you are loved and cherished by God?

. . . .

Father God, please take away my shame so that I can be free to be who You want me to be.

THE DREAM MAKER

*"What no eye has seen, what no ear has heard,
and what no human mind has conceived"—the
things God has prepared for those who love him.*

1 CORINTHIANS 2:9 NIV

You probably have a whole bunch of dreams and goals. You know that some of them may be impossible to achieve, but you love to think about them anyway. Other goals might be things you're confident you can achieve if you work hard enough. Disappointment can rear its ugly head, though, when what you wanted— what you expected—doesn't happen like you thought it would or doesn't happen as fast as you had planned.

But God knows your dreams, and He shares them. He created you and knows what you can do even better than you know yourself. So maintain your commitment to your goals, but keep your focus on the dream maker instead of the dream itself. And let God share the excitement when a dream comes true.

. . . .

*Thank You for giving me dreams, Lord.
Show me how to give them back to You.*

NORMAL LiFE

"I am with you, and I will protect you wherever you go. . . . I will not leave you until I have finished giving you everything I have promised you."

<small>GENESIS 28:15 NLT</small>

When you're going through a hard time of some sort, you may keep wishing that life would just get back to "normal." And then, just when you think you're back to your old routines, able to calm down and enjoy life again, something *else* hits your life, another crisis that blows your "normal life" to smithereens.

You may need to accept that crises *are* normal life. Big and little challenges will always be a part of life. It could be a fight with your best friend or a pandemic; it might be a failing grade on a school project or a death in your family. But you don't have to fall into a deep depression over any of these things. Instead, you can reread the promises God gives you in the Bible, trusting that no matter what happens, He will be with you. He will get you through every crisis you ever face.

. . . .

Father God, teach me to accept life's challenges, knowing that You will give me strength to overcome them.

TiME WiTH GOD

Draw near to God, and he will draw near to you.
JAMES 4:8 NRSV

If you find yourself feeling swamped with discouragement, take a look at your life and try to remember the last time you really focused on God. If you realize He seems far away, there's a pretty good chance you haven't been spending much time with Him. Of course, God hasn't gone anywhere. He's as close to you as ever, surrounding you with His love. But all the stress and worries, commitments and responsibilities of your daily life may have blinded your spiritual vision.

If you find yourself in this situation, try setting aside a quiet morning or evening (a time when you're not likely to be interrupted) to spend alone with God. Go for a walk with Him. Read the Bible. Read a book that gives you new ideas about life. Listen to music. Journal. Pray. Take time to catch up with God (and with yourself).

* *

Thank You, Lord, that You are always with me.
Remind me when I need to spend more time with You.

PREJUDICE

In Christ's family there can be no division. . . .
Among us you are all equal.
GALATIANS 3:28 MSG

If you love and follow Jesus, there's no room in your life for prejudice. He came to unite everyone in Him, not separate us according to the color of our skin, our gender, or anything else about us. You may not think you're prejudiced in any way, but everyone has blind spots, things about themselves they don't realize are there.

So take time to consider if there are groups of people you think are less intelligent, less worthy, less *anything*. Ask God to show you any beliefs or attitudes you've been keeping hidden from yourself. We are all equal in God's eyes, and He wants us to work together to build a world where no one has to face prejudice and discrimination.

. . . .

Please show me, Lord, any prejudice that I haven't
wanted to face in myself, and show me how to work
with You to fight prejudice wherever it exists.

ACCEPTING AND GIVING HELP

*"You will surely wear out. . .because the task is
too heavy for you; you cannot do it alone."*

EXODUS 18:18 NASB

The Bible talks about the body of Christ because God
knows we need each other in order to grow and serve
Him. The body of Christ is all the people of God, working together to serve Him. But sometimes it can be
hard to admit you need help. You don't want to bother
anyone. You don't want people to think you're needy
or silly. And you don't want to feel as though you're
not in control of your own life.

But the truth is nobody can make it through life
without the help of others. Sometimes you may need
more help, sometimes less. If it's your turn to need
help today, one day it will be your turn to help others.
We don't have to face our problems alone!

*Jesus, I'm so glad I belong to Your body. Teach me to
accept help—and show me opportunities to help others.*

GOD CAN TURN IT AROUND!

*Every detail in our lives of love for God
is worked into something good.*
ROMANS 8:28 MSG

God can take absolutely everything that happens in your life and use it to create something good. That includes the sad times, the hard times, the embarrassing times, and the frustrating times. If you read the accounts recorded in the Bible, you'll see that again and again, God took impossible situations and turned them into something else. Read about Daniel, who was thrown into a lions' den (the book of Daniel, chapter 6); Joseph, whose brothers were so jealous they tried to kill him (Genesis 37 and 39); and the Israelites, who were starving in the desert (Exodus 16). All these people were in terrible situations, and yet God used their circumstances to bring new blessings into their lives.

What are you facing that seems impossible? What situation appears hopeless? What circumstance is overwhelming you? God can turn it around, just like He did for Daniel, Joseph, the Israelites, and countless others!

* *

*Thank You, Father God, that You are using
every single detail in my life to bless me and
build something wonderful in my life.*

BRINGING OUT THE BEST IN OTHERS

You can show others the goodness of God, for he called you out of the darkness into his wonderful light.

1 PETER 2:9 NLT

Peter, who wrote this verse, was one of Jesus' close friends, and he knew firsthand what it was like to be called out of the darkness into the light. When Peter first began to follow Jesus, he was always saying stupid things. He got angry easily. He liked to boast, but then he couldn't live up to his big claims. But Jesus saw past all of Peter's flaws and mistakes. He saw what Peter could be, the person God had created him to be.

God treats you the same way that Jesus treated Peter, and God also wants you to have His same attitude toward the people in your life. Instead of focusing on all the things that bug you in people, try looking for what is good in them. The more attention you pay to the good in others, the more you will encourage them to be the people God wants them to be.

. . . .

Teach me, Lord Jesus, to see others the way You do.

GOD IS YOUR STRENGTH

*Whom have I in heaven but you? And earth
has nothing I desire besides you. My flesh and
my heart may fail, but God is the strength
of my heart and my portion forever.*

PSALM 73:25–26 NIV

You don't always have to be strong. It's okay to admit that you're tired or scared or tempted. Share your feelings with God—and He will help you. He won't get mad because you're not perfect or invincible. Of course, He might not magically remove you from the situation, but He *will* show you how to get through it. Maybe He'll lead you to exactly what you need to read in the Bible or another book, something that will help you see things a little differently. He may want to use another person to help you, so don't be afraid to tell someone else that you have a problem.

Rely on God. One step at a time, one day at a time, He will give you the strength you need to face every challenge that comes your way.

*Father God, I'm depending on You to get me
through. Show me if there's anything You want
me to do that will help me solve my problems.*

REAL FREEDOM

Do not turn your freedom into an opportunity for the flesh, but serve one another through love.

GALATIANS 5:13 NASB

Jesus has set you free—free from the past, free from fear, free from bad habits, free to be the real you. But the freedom you have in Jesus doesn't mean you can do anything you want to do now. It wouldn't be wise to say, "Now that I'm following Jesus, I don't have to worry about making mistakes or hurting people, because I know that He will always forgive me. He'll take any mistake I make and turn it around into something good." While there's some truth in that, the whole point of following Jesus is that you're trying to be like Him. Jesus never put Himself ahead of others; He spent His life helping and healing others. So don't mistake the freedom He has given you as a chance to go on being selfish. Let love rule your life. That's the best way to follow Jesus and enjoy the real freedom He gives.

. . . .

I want to learn how to be more like You, Jesus. Please teach me what I need to know, and may Your Spirit live in me and guide me so that I'm filled with love for You and others.

HOPE

*Blessed be the Lord—day after day he carries
us along. He's our Savior, our God, oh yes!
He's God-for-us, he's God-who-saves-us.
Lord GOD knows all death's ins and outs.*

PSALM 68:19–20 MSG

The Bible often talks about hope. You may think of
hope as being like a wish or that being hopeful is the
same as expecting something good to happen. The
Bible's kind of hope, though, is far greater and deeper
than that. Hope is what David was expressing when he
wrote these verses. God will never stop helping you;
God will save you from all that has trapped you and
held you back from becoming who He wants you to
be; God is always on your side; and finally, God not
only will be with you all through your life but also will
be with you when you pass through death. This kind
of hope means that even though you don't know what
the future holds, you're not afraid; you know God will
always be with you. No matter where the road ahead
takes you, it always leads you into His presence.

- -

*You, Lord, are the reason I can
face the future with hope.*

FOCUS ON GOD!

Don't copy the behavior and customs of this world, but let God transform you into a new person by changing the way you think. Then you will learn to know God's will for you, which is good and pleasing and perfect.

ROMANS 12:2 NLT

The culture you live in has different ideas about what's important in life than what the Bible teaches. It's all too easy for your values to get bent out of shape, sometimes even without you realizing what has happened. Your focus shifts away from God. You want to control your own life, and when things turn out differently than you hoped, you feel as though God let you down. You forget that God's job is not to make your life easy and grant all your wishes. Instead, God is calling you to work with Him to build a world where love rules. He wants you to build your life on enjoying His love and loving Him back in return, while at the same time sharing His love with everyone in your circle of influence.

. . . .

Teach me, Father God, to understand what You want for my life, and remind me not to let my ideas get bent out of shape by the culture in which I live.

FOLLOWING JESUS

And over all these virtues put on love,
which binds them all together in perfect unity.

COLOSSIANS 3:14 NIV

Many different things are involved in following Jesus. As you read the Bible or listen in church or Sunday school, you might start to feel confused or overwhelmed. It may seem a little like learning to drive—as though it's just too hard to remember what your feet are supposed to do at the same time that your hands and eyes are doing what they're supposed to do.

But when it comes to following Jesus, one thing pulls it all together and helps you know what to do—and that's love. If you're not sure what to say to someone, ask yourself what love would say. If you're uncertain what choice to make, ask yourself which is the most loving choice. This is the one rule Jesus gave us: to love God, each other, and ourselves (Mark 12:30–31). Love makes sense of everything else—so that you can "drive" freely and easily.

· ·

If I start feeling proud of myself, Lord Jesus,
but I'm not being kind to other people, remind
me that love is Your commandment.

TAKING ACTION

*When Naomi heard in Moab that the L*ORD *had*
come to the aid of his people by providing
food for them, she and her daughters-in-
law prepared to return home from there.

RUTH 1:6 NIV

Naomi was from Bethlehem, and now that her husband
and her sons had died, she wanted to leave the home
she had made in Moab and go back to the place where
she grew up. She had been gone many years, and by
now Moab must have seemed like home; but when
she heard God was opening up new opportunities in
her homeland, she decided to go. She didn't just sit
around hoping God would somehow take care of her
and her daughters-in-law. She took action.

The Bible is full of stories like Ruth and Naomi's,
stories about women who found new lives because
God helped them. In this story, Naomi's daughter-in-
law Ruth married a Jewish man. This woman from a
foreign land became one of Jesus' ancestors. When
Naomi heard a message about what God was doing,
she made up her mind and took action—and her action
ultimately led to the birth of Jesus! What action might
God be calling you to take in your life?

. . . .

Lord Jesus, please show me any opportunities
You want me to take. Show me how to act in
ways that point to You and Your goodness.

WAKE UP!

*Then Jacob awoke from his sleep and said, "Surely the
LORD is in this place, and I wasn't even aware of it!"*
GENESIS 28:16 NLT

Do you ever find yourself walking through your life like
a sleepwalker, barely aware of what's going on? You're
getting your schoolwork done, talking to your friends,
doing all the things that are expected of you, but you
feel like something has frozen or gone numb inside you.
If you occasionally have feelings like this, don't worry.
You're normal! (But if those feelings last longer than
a few days, you should tell an adult you trust who can
help you figure out what's going on.) Usually, sooner
or later, God will send something along to wake you
up. Then, like Jacob in this Bible verse, you'll say, "Oh,
God was here with me all along! I just didn't know."
God's presence in your life doesn't depend on your
feelings. Whether you're sleeping or wide awake, He's
always there.

. . . .

*When I "fall asleep" spiritually or emotionally, Lord
God, wake me up so I can feel You with me once more.*

SING!

Come, let's shout praises to God. . . .
Let's march into his presence singing praises,
lifting the rafters with our hymns!
PSALM 95:1–2 MSG

David, who wrote most of the book of Psalms, was a king of Israel, but he didn't have an easy life. He made some pretty bad mistakes in his life. He also made some pretty bad enemies. At one point, he ended up hiding in a cave so his enemies wouldn't find him and kill him. The apostle Paul, who wrote many of the books in the New Testament, also had his share of troubles. He was arrested and thrown in jail, not once but three times. And yet both David and Paul literally sang with joy because of all God had done for them.

It's not easy to sing when all you want to do is cry. But singing can lift your sadness. Researchers have even found that singing takes away depression and anxiety and creates feelings of hope and happiness; it can even give you new energy when you're exhausted.

So the next time you're sad or discouraged or tired, play your favorite music and sing to God. He loves to hear your voice!

Remind me, Father God, to sing
more and complain less.

IN THE BELLY OF A FISH

*"When my life was ebbing away, I remembered you,
Lord, and my prayer rose to you, to your holy temple."*

JONAH 2:7 NIV

God asked Jonah to go share His love with the people of Nineveh, but Jonah had too much prejudice against those people. He didn't want to help them, and he refused to go where God sent him. As a result, he ended up inside the belly of a great fish. Try to imagine what that must have been like. Dark, wet, smelly, slimy. The consequences of Jonah's choices couldn't have been much worse.

And yet God was still with Jonah, still listening for his prayers. God didn't say to Jonah, "Too bad, you had your chance, but you blew it, so now you're just going to have to be digested by an enormous fish." God gave Jonah another chance. And this time, Jonah took it. He went to Nineveh and shared God's love.

. . . .

*I'm sorry for the times I don't want to listen
to You, Lord God. Thank You that You give me
second (and third and fourth) chances.*

DREAMS

He had a dream in which he saw a stairway resting on the earth, with its top reaching to heaven, and the angels of God were ascending and descending on it.

GENESIS 28:12 NIV

Jacob was having some pretty bad family problems—so bad that he ran away. When he stopped for the night, he must have been feeling discouraged and afraid. But right there, in the middle of still another impossible situation, God gave Jacob a dream. In the dream, Jacob saw that this world was connected to heaven by a shining stairway, and the angels were constantly going back and forth between earth and heaven. The dream didn't seem to change anything, at least not on the outside—Jacob's brother was still mad at him—but it changed Jacob on the inside. It made him see his life in a new way.

God might want to talk to you through your dreams too. After all, He is just as much the God of the nighttime as He is of the daytime. So ask God to use your dreams to give you new insights into your life. Pay attention to your dreams.

. . . .

Father God, I want to hear what You're saying to me. Please use other people, the books I read, the world of nature, and even my dreams to get Your messages through to me.

OPEN DOORS

*"I know all the things you do, and I have opened a door
for you that no one can close. You have little strength,
yet you obeyed my word and did not deny me."*

REVELATION 3:8 NLT

In the book of Revelation, Jesus promises the church at Philadelphia that He has new opportunities in store for them—an open door that no one can close. Notice He doesn't yell at the church for being weak; instead, He praises the church for its commitment to Him, despite its weakness.

You too can claim Jesus' message in this verse. As the apostle Paul said, "That is why, for Christ's sake, I delight in weaknesses, in insults, in hardships, in persecutions, in difficulties. For when I am weak, then I am strong" (2 Corinthians 12:10 NIV). When you stop trying to be in control of your life and give everything to God, that is the very moment God will make you strong. Jesus has new doors to open for you, doors that will lead you into amazing opportunities and thrilling adventures. When you follow Jesus, He promises that nothing and no one can keep you from walking through the doors He opens.

. . . .

Thank You, Jesus, for opening new doors in my life.

HELPLESS

I am content with weaknesses. . . .
For when I am weak, then I am strong.
2 CORINTHIANS 12:10 ESV

You've probably heard the expression "God helps those who help themselves." There's a certain truth to the saying (God doesn't want you to sit there expecting a miracle when He's already put the means to accomplish something into your hands), but the opposite is also true: God helps those who are helpless. Remember poor Jonah in the belly of the great fish! Think about the Israelites who were slaves in Egypt. Or read the story about the baby Moses, who was in danger of being killed (see the book of Exodus, chapter 2). Again and again, God rescues people who have no way of helping themselves. In the middle of impossible situations, He opens doors that lead to safety, freedom, and joy.

And He'll do the same for you!

When I'm helpless, Lord God, please help me the way You helped Jonah, the Israelites, baby Moses, and so many other people. Remind me that because of You, my situation is never hopeless.

WHAT'S ON THE INSIDE

Don't be concerned about the outward beauty of fancy hairstyles, expensive jewelry, or beautiful clothes. You should clothe yourselves instead with the beauty that comes from within, the unfading beauty of a gentle and quiet spirit, which is so precious to God.

1 PETER 3:3–4 NLT

As a young woman, you may find yourself worrying about your appearance. God wants you to take care of your body—and your hairstyle, clothes, jewelry, and makeup can all be ways to care for your wonderful body. But God is far more concerned with what is on the inside of you, in your heart and mind. He wants you to wear the beautiful "clothes" that come from being gentle to others and from trusting in Him. This is the kind of beauty that lasts forever. It doesn't matter if you're wearing your most raggedy sweats, your hair is dirty, and you have a giant pimple on the tip of your nose—you can still be truly beautiful.

• •

Help me to keep my priorities straight, Lord, spending more time on being a loving person than on trying to get my clothes, hair, and makeup just right.

ENJOY!

Seize life! Eat bread with gusto. . . . Oh yes—
God takes pleasure in your pleasure! Dress
festively every morning. Don't skimp on colors
and scarves. Relish life. . .each and every day of
your precarious life. Each day is God's gift.

ECCLESIASTES 9:7–9 MSG

Like a loving mother, God loves to feed His children. He loves to see them happy, enjoying all the good things He has created. So don't be afraid to take pleasure in the life He has given you. Put on your best clothes! Have fun with your friends! Eat something delicious! Your enjoyment of these things can bring you even closer to God, so long as you remember that all of life's pleasures come from Him. Start each day with the attitude that it's a gift from God, the one who loves you so much—and then say thank You all day long!

Lord God, thank You for my life. May each
thing I enjoy bring me closer to You.

SPREAD ENCOURAGEMENT

Therefore encourage one another and build each other up, just as in fact you are doing.

1 THESSALONIANS 5:11 NIV

Encouragement is more than words. It is also valuing the other person, being tolerant of their flaws, doing whatever you can to help them, and praying for them. Encouragement includes looking for whatever is good in a person and pointing it out. Encouragement means forgiving and asking for forgiveness. It asks that you hold out a helping hand when you recognize someone's weaknesses. Encouragement always builds others up instead of tearing them down.

Today, pay attention to the people around you. Who could use some encouragement? (Probably everybody!)

Thank You, Lord Jesus, that I am part of Your body, a living organism where each part depends on all the other parts. Show me how to encourage and support others in Your body.

COMPLIMENT MORE THAN YOU CRITICIZE

Gently encourage the stragglers, and reach out for the exhausted, pulling them to their feet. Be patient with each person, attentive to individual needs. . . . Look for the best in each other, and always do your best to bring it out.

1 THESSALONIANS 5:14–15 MSG

If you see someone who is struggling (maybe they're using drugs or alcohol or hurting themself in other ways, or maybe they're acting violent or mean), God doesn't want you to judge that person. He also doesn't want you to gossip with your friends about them. That person, no matter how ugly and messed up they may seem on the outside, is precious to God.

That's why He asks that when you have a chance, you reach out your hands to help and encourage. Focus on what is good in that person, and do your best to strengthen that in them. Compliment more than you criticize. As you shift your attention to lifting them up rather than dragging them down, you will be showing them God's love—and that's exactly what they need most to heal and grow.

* *

When I catch myself judging and criticizing, Lord Jesus, remind me that You want me to show Your love to everyone.

FILLED WITH LOVE

Imitate God, therefore, in everything you do,
because you are his dear children. Live a life filled
with love, following the example of Christ.
EPHESIANS 5:1–2 NLT

God knows you're not perfect. He doesn't expect you to be. He's not up in heaven waiting to squash you with a "giant thumb" every time you make a mistake. He doesn't look for opportunities to say, "Now look what you did! Boy, did you mess up this time!" Instead, He is always seeking to encourage you and to help you grow (the same way He wants you to encourage others).

And as you get to know God better, imitating Him more and more closely, you *will* grow. You'll become more like Him—living a life that's filled with love, a life that loves so much that it gives itself away.

. . . .

Teach me, Lord Jesus, to be like You.
May everything I do and say come from love.
Help me grow into the person You want me to be.

SCRIPTURE INDEX

MORE ENCOURAGEMENT FOR YOUR BEAUTIFUL SPIRIT!

You Belong
Devotions and Prayers for a Teen Girl's Heart

*You Were Created with Purpose by a Loving, Heavenly Creator. . .
You Belong!*

This delightful devotional is a lovely reminder of that you were created with purpose by a heavenly Creator. . .and that you belong—right here and now—in this world. 180 encouraging readings and inspiring prayers, rooted in biblical truth, will reassure your uncertain heart, helping you to understand that you're never alone and always loved. In each devotional reading, you will encounter the bountiful blessings and grace of your Creator, while coming to trust His purposeful plan for you in this world.

Flexible Casebound / 978-1-63609-169-3